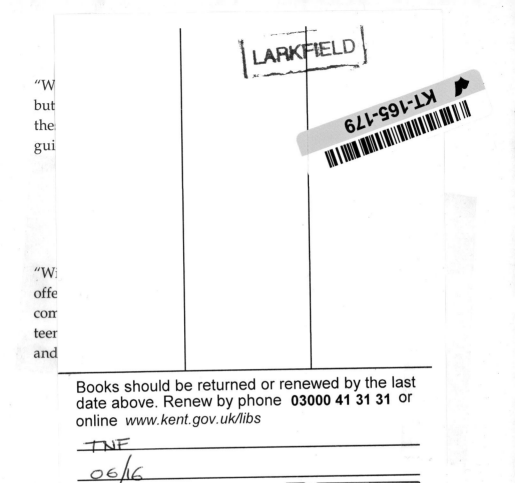
"W
but
the
gui

"Wi
offe
com
teer
and

"Th
cogn
offer
Teens can easily recognize themselves in this book and become
empowered to overcome their anxiety."

—**Karen Lynn Cassiday, PhD**, managing director at
The Anxiety Treatment Center of Greater Chicago
and clinical assistant professor at Rosalind Franklin
Univer

"*The Anxiety Survival Guide for Teens* by Jennifer Shannon is a clear, concise, helpful guide with all the key tools to help you overcome your anxiety. Why suffer another day from anxiety when you can use these tools right now? Each chapter gives you powerful and easy-to-understand self-help tools to overcome the many difficulties that teens will face. I will recommend this to my colleagues and clients."

> —**Robert L. Leahy, PhD**, director of the American Institute for Cognitive Therapy in New York, NY, and author of *The Worry Cure: Seven Steps to Stop Worry from Stopping You*

"All parents want to lift the burden of stress from their teen's shoulders, but many teens don't want to talk about it. They do, however, desperately want to feel better. In a completely clear, accessible, and engaging way, Jennifer Shannon's *Anxiety Survival Guide for Teens* tells teens exactly what they need to do to help themselves do just that. The simple exercises in this book teach teens how to break free from their anxiety and see themselves and their lives in a whole new light—a more realistic one. Every teen will benefit from the strategies Ms. Shannon provides. I highly recommend this wonderful book!"

> —**Tamar Chansky, PhD**, author of *Freeing Your Child from Anxiety* and *Freeing Yourself from Anxiety: 4 Simple Steps to Overcome Worry and Create the Life You Want*

"Relief is on the way for anxious teens. *The Anxiety Survival Guide for Teens* teaches proven steps to uncover the causes and learn what to do to manage anxiety. Unlike many similar books, this guide addresses all types of anxiety with drawings and helpful stories about common situations faced by teens and young adults. Whether mildly or super anxious, complete the exercises in this book to get a grip on your anxiety."

—**Christine A. Padesky, PhD**, psychologist
and coauthor of *Mind Over Mood*

the *i n s t a n t* h e l p
s o l u t i o n s   s e r i e s

Young people today need mental health resources more than ever. That's why New Harbinger created the **Instant Help Solutions Series** especially for teens. Written by leading psychologists, physicians, and professionals, these evidence-based self-help books offer practical tips and strategies for dealing with a variety of mental health issues and life challenges teens face, such as depression, anxiety, bullying, eating disorders, trauma, and self-esteem problems.

Studies have shown that young people who learn healthy coping skills early on are better able to navigate problems later in life. Engaging and easy-to-use, these books provide teens with the tools they need to thrive—at home, at school, and on into adulthood.

This series is part of the **New Harbinger Instant Help Books** imprint, founded by renowned child psychologist Lawrence Shapiro. For a complete list of books in this series, visit newharbinger.com.

the anxiety survival guide for teens

CBT skills to overcome fear, worry & panic

JENNIFER SHANNON, LMFT
ILLUSTRATIONS BY DOUG SHANNON

Instant Help Books
An Imprint of New Harbinger Publications, Inc.

Publisher's Note

"Getting Extra Help: Therapy and Medication" adapted from The Shyness and Social Anxiety Workbook for Teens by Jennifer Shannon. Used by permission of New Harbinger Publications, Inc.

Distributed in Canada by Raincoast Books

Copyright © 2015 by Jennifer Shannon
     Instant Help Books
     An Imprint of New Harbinger Publications, Inc.
     5674 Shattuck Avenue
     Oakland, CA 94609
     www.newharbinger.com

Illustrations by Doug Shannon; Cover design by Amy Shoup; Acquired by Tesilya Hanauer; Edited by Susan LaCroix

Library of Congress Cataloging-in-Publication Data

Shannon, Jennifer.
 The anxiety survival guide for teens : CBT skills to overcome fear, worry, and panic / Jennifer Shannon ; illustrated by Doug Shannon.
  pages cm. -- (The instant help solutions series)
 ISBN 978-1-62625-243-1 (paperback) -- ISBN 978-1-62625-244-8 (pdf e-book) -- ISBN 978-1-62625-245-5 (epub) 1. Anxiety--Juvenile literature. 2. Cognitive therapy for teenagers--Problems exercises, etc. I. Shannon, Doug, editor. II. Title.
 BF575.A6S475 2015
 155.5'1246--dc23

        2015007029

Printed in the United States of America

17 16 15

10 9 8 7 6 5 4 3 2

To my mentors: Michael Tompkins, whose brilliant guidance helped me to build my foundation in CBT; Christine Padesky, whose wisdom and clear voice has helped me to find my own; and Jacqueline Persons, who always helps me see the big picture.

Contents

Introduction

You Are Not Alone and You Are Not to Blame

Teens who suffer from anxiety often think of themselves as weak, stupid, or any of many other negative labels. You may think you are the only one who feels things this way and that everyone else is normal.

The thing is, normal doesn't exist. Everyone feels anxiety, and in a surprising variety of situations. Some feel it in a crowded cafeteria, others in an empty hall. Many people panic giving an oral report while others feel panic at random times for no apparent reason. The star quarterback who shouts audibles loud enough to be heard above the roaring crowd may get so anxious around the girl he's attracted to that he is unable to string two words together. Depending on the situation, almost everyone can feel overwhelmed with anxiety.

There are anxious teens all around you. Studies show that anxiety is the most common mental health problem in America, affecting nearly one in five people. If you are sitting in a classroom of thirty students, chances are that at least a row of you are suffering from one of the seven most common varieties of anxiety: social anxiety, generalized anxiety, separation anxiety, obsessive-compulsive disorder, specific phobias, panic, and agoraphobia. The reason you are unaware of your anxious peers is that they are just as good at hiding their anxiety as you are.

You are not alone, and you are also not to blame. Scientists who study DNA have isolated a number of genes associated with heightened or lowered sensitivity to danger, including genes that have been nicknamed the "warrior/worrier gene" and the "risk-taking gene." Your present level of anxiety is partially inherited. In fact, if you have a parent or sibling with an anxiety disorder you are four times as likely to suffer from anxiety yourself.

In addition to your genetic makeup, your level of anxiety can be influenced by a traumatic life experience or your parents' anxious behavior. So blaming yourself for your anxiety makes about as much sense as blaming yourself for the color of your eyes, things that have happened to you, or the family you were born into. You can't change your genetics, your life experience, or your parents. These are the cards you were dealt. But will you have to suffer with anxiety for the rest of your life, missing out on things you want to do? Are millions of anxious teens predestined to become anxious adults? Absolutely not! You *can* learn how to manage your anxiety, so that you can do the things that are important to you. This book will show you how.

Here is a brief overview of the different types of anxiety this book addresses. You can also download a brief quiz that will help you identify which types of anxiety you suffer from at http://www.newharbinger.com/32431. (See the very back of this book for more information about downloads.) Don't be surprised if there is more than one; that's very common. Later chapters in this book will focus in more detail on how to deal with your specific types of anxiety.

Generalized Anxiety

- Frequent worry about school, your health or the health of your loved ones, or bad things happening in the world

- Feeling tense or restless, having difficulty concentrating, or having trouble falling asleep at night due to worry

- Frequent stomachaches, headaches, or muscle tension

Phobias

- Fear and avoidance of elevators, heights, storms, or water

- Fear of certain animals or insects

- Unreasonable fear of needles, blood, choking, or vomiting

Social Anxiety

- Uncomfortable shyness or fear of doing or saying something embarrassing

- Panic when having to give an oral presentation or be the center of attention

- Difficulty starting or joining in conversations with others

Panic Attacks

- Feeling frightened suddenly or for no apparent reason

- Racing heart, trouble breathing, or dizziness

- Strange, detached feeling, as if things are not real

Agoraphobia

- Avoidance or fear of going into situations in which you have panicked before

- Fear of being trapped in places like cars and planes, or fear of going into tunnels or over bridges

- Fear of suddenly having to go to the bathroom but being trapped or far away, so that you cannot get there in time

Obsessive-Compulsive Disorder

- Frequent intrusive or unpleasant thoughts

- Fear and doubt about illness, germs, harming yourself or others, offending God, your sexual identity, or losing or forgetting things

- Need to know, or for things to be just right

Separation Anxiety

- Avoiding being away from home or people who are important to you

- Worry that something terrible might happen to people who are important to you when you are away from them

- Frequent calling or texting to make sure people you care about are okay

Now you have a better idea of the different types of anxiety. I hope you don't feel overwhelmed by this list. Sometimes names and labels can feel scary, especially if you are anxious to begin with. You may be thinking that this means there is something really wrong with you.

There is nothing wrong with you that you can't fix. The purpose of naming the types of anxiety you may suffer from is to give you specific and powerful tools that will help you manage your anxiety and gain confidence to live the life you want. But before you jump to the chapters that focus on your type—or types—of anxiety, let's look at what all anxious teens have in common.

Part 1

Chapter 1

The Monkey Mind

Staying Alive

One summer day about thirty thousand years ago, three young Cro-Magnon hunters were following reindeer tracks across a rocky plateau when they spotted their prey grazing on a patch of grass near a lone tree. They crouched down low and crept forward, gripping their spears in anticipation. Just as the hunters were closing in, they heard a faint rustle behind them. When they turned their heads they saw a saber-toothed tiger bearing down upon them. The terrified hunters bolted, and so did the deer. All three hunters made it back to camp. The deer wasn't so lucky.

One thing, at least, has not changed in thirty thousand years. Whether it is a charging saber-toothed tiger on a prehistoric plain or a car running a red light when you are crossing an intersection, the human reaction is instantaneous. Our brains are hardwired for survival. Your brain's number one job is staying alive.

Your brain tells your body when to relax and when to respond to danger. When there is danger your nervous system acts in an instant, before you have time to form thoughts or make plans—like a smoke detector in your house that sounds the alarm before you can smell the smoke. It's called the *fight-or-flight response*, and we share it not only with deer but with all creatures that have a brain.

> *The next day the three hungry hunters set out again in search of prey and again they found some reindeer tracks. They weren't following the trail very long, however, before they spotted several tiger prints. The first hunter grunted and kept going, apparently unconcerned. The second hunter spun around and ran back to camp. The third hunter wiped his brow and took a few deep breaths. He was anxious, but he was also hungry. After studying the direction of the tracks, he headed off in the opposite direction. Shortly afterward, he speared a deer. He was the hero in the tales of the day's hunt told by the fire that night.*

Even when there is no imminent threat, your brain is still looking for danger. Although you are usually unaware of it, a primitive part of your brain is constantly scanning your surroundings, remembering past events and looking into the future, deciding what is safe for you to do and what is not.

Although neuroscientists are learning new things all the time about how that part of the brain works, it is still a mystery exactly how we decide which risks to take, and why our decisions vary so much from person to person.

The "fearless" hunter who ignored the tracks continued on the trail and wound up being killed by the tiger. The hunter who was made anxious by the tracks, and changed his plans accordingly, survived and thrived. Being able to feel some anxiety, even when there is no immediate threat, can help you make good decisions and stay alive. But what about the hunter who turned and ran even though there was no tiger present and thus no imminent danger?

The following day the most anxious hunter, embarrassed because he had run away the previous day, joined a hunting party, determined to make good of himself. But every rustling of a leaf sounded like a tiger; every footprint on the ground looked like a tiger track. Just thinking about the tiger made the hunter's heart beat fast and his stomach turn, almost as if a tiger was right there in front of him. He slowed down the

hunting party so much that he was left behind. In the tales of the hunt by the fire that night his name wasn't mentioned.

Feeling more anxiety than a situation calls for is certainly not adaptive. It stops you from doing what you want and need to do—which, in our anxious hunter's case, was bringing home meat for his family and tribe.

The anxious hunter's problem, and yours, is that fight-or-flight responses feel real whether there is real danger or not. If your brain reacts to a situation as dangerous—even if it's not—your nervous system will act accordingly, making your heart beat like a drum, your skin break out in sweat, your fingers tingle, your stomach nauseous, your throat constricted, and your head spin. The system is sounding false alarms, like a smoke detector that goes off every time you make a piece of toast.

Regardless of what else you are doing, this system keeps humming away in the background. If you are genetically—or for whatever reason—extra sensitive to threats, you are likely getting lots of alerts warning you about bad things about to happen. I like to think of this part of the brain as the *monkey mind*. Its relentless stream of scary thoughts is like a frightened monkey's chatter.

The story of the three hunters illustrates an important point about anxiety: it is not the situation that triggers how we feel and what we do, but rather *what we think* about the situation. When a wildly threat–sensitive monkey with a loud alarm is doing the thinking, its scary chatter keeps setting off false alarms, filling you with anxiety that stops you from going where you want to go and being who you want to be.

This book will show you how to stop your monkey mind from ruling your life—how to make choices that are not dictated by fear. You will learn to identify monkey chatter, ignore false alarms, and take back control of your life. After all, there is more to living than just staying alive. You can live the life you want to live!

Chapter 2

Monkey Logic

Understanding the Avoidance Cycle

Justin was a fifteen-year-old who loved skateboarding. He rode his skateboard to school and to his friends' houses, and he spent as much time as he could at the skate park. One day he was on his way home from skating with his friends when an off-leash dog in a park began to chase him. Justin was listening to music on his headphones and he didn't hear the dog approaching. When the dog caught up to him it knocked him off his skateboard. The dog's owner quickly appeared and pulled the dog away, apologizing repeatedly. Justin wasn't bitten, but he felt like he could have been. He told the dog's owner he was okay, but he walked home bruised and shaken.

The next day, Justin was skateboarding to school when he spotted a neighbor walking her large dog, coming directly toward him. He felt his heart begin to beat fast and was aware of feeling panic, similar to how he felt the day before. Justin stopped skating and picked up his board. He was only a block from home, so he decided to walk back and catch a ride to school from one of his parents. As soon as the front door shut and he was back in his house he felt much calmer.

The situation that morning was the same one Justin had encountered many times before, skateboarding to school past a woman walking her dog. The dog had always been well-behaved in the past. What triggered his sudden fight-or-flight response?

If you asked Justin, he might have answered, "I don't know. The dog just made me nervous." All Justin was aware of was feeling anxious at the sight of the dog and feeling calmer when he turned back. But whether he was aware of it or not, his monkey mind interpreted the situation that morning with a new twist.

Because of his experience with the other dog the day before, and because Justin happens to have an oversensitive-to-threat nervous system, Justin's monkey had a new thought about this dog on a leash, a thought that triggered a wave of anxiety: *What if that dog gets off its leash and attacks you?*

If Justin had taken a few deep breaths, reminded himself that the dog was on a leash and that it had never been aggressive before, and kept on skating, that would probably have been the end of the story. But Justin's anxiety hit him hard. It felt like a real threat. He did what all anxious teens do when they feel overwhelmed by anxious feelings in a situation: he avoided it.

When the monkey mind's interpretation of a situation is accepted as true, it always leads to avoidance.

SITUATION + (ANXIOUS THOUGHT) + ANXIOUS FEELING = AVOIDANCE

Justin's decision to let his parents drive him to school may seem like an overreaction to us. After all, the dog was on a leash and not dangerous. But from Justin's point of view it made perfect sense. His monkey mind's interpretation of the dog as a threat triggered anxiety for him, and nobody wants to feel anxious. Avoidance is the behavior of choice for all the types of anxiety that we talk about in this book, even the ones that don't appear to have anything to do with avoiding things. Avoidance is the behavior of choice because it lowers your anxiety quickly.

> The next day when Justin reached for his skateboard, he felt a little wave of anxiety. He wondered whether he might run into that dog again. So, just to be safe, he had his parents drive him to school again.

Avoidance works so fast and so well, you'll want to use it again. The problem is that with repeated use, avoidance has a nasty side effect: *The more you avoid a situation, the scarier that situation becomes.*

Avoiding dogs was keeping Justin calm, but it wasn't reducing his anxiety about dogs. All he had to do was think about skateboarding and he felt anxious about dogs. Avoidance was making his anxiety worse and keeping him from doing what he loved.

The reason your anxiety gets worse is that your monkey mind always assumes that it was the action you just did that prevented something bad from happening. When Justin's monkey saw that he was in the house and that he was not bitten by the dog, it concluded that *Justin was not attacked by the dog because he went into the house.*

You might be asking why the monkey mind would keep on with the same chatter, even when it is wrong. Doesn't it ever question anything or take a second look at a situation before setting off your alarms? No. The monkey mind has only one mission: keeping you safe. And if you are an anxious person, you have a monkey that is hyperactive and hypersensitive to danger. It cannot tell the difference between imagined and realistic threats. Its anxious thoughts are not carefully considered; they are only wild guesses.

When you avoid a situation because of anxiety, you are, in effect, agreeing with the monkey logic that the situation was dangerous. You are training your monkey mind to make the same interpretation next time, make the same chatter, and sound the alarm.

You may not think what you are doing is avoiding anything. Is worrying, for example, avoiding? Yes! When you are thinking about a problem, running it over and over in your mind, you are looking for a solution that will enable you to *not* feel anxious. You are avoiding actually *feeling* the anxiety that problem brings up.

Let's look at how monkey logic and avoiding anxiety works with anxiety types other than Justin's.

Monkey thought: *What if you are late to class? Being late would be a disaster. You would get detention.*

Avoidant behavior: Rush to get ready for school and leave fifteen minutes early.

Monkey logic: *Because you left early you did not get detention.*

Monkey thought: *What if you get the stomach flu? There is nothing worse than throwing up. You can't handle it.*

Avoidant behavior: Avoid people who might be ill.

Monkey logic: *Because you avoided sick people, you did not throw up.*

Monkey thought: *What if people think you are boring? People will laugh at you or talk about you, and you will make a bad impression.*

Avoidant behavior: Avoid initiating conversations.

Monkey logic: *Because you were quiet, no one found out you are boring.*

Monkey thought: *What if you get a panic attack? If you have a panic attack it might not ever stop, or you might die.*

Avoidant behavior: Avoid situations in which you have had a panic attack before.

Monkey logic: *Because you avoided these situations you did not panic, lose control, or die.*

Monkey thought: *What if something terrible happens to someone you love?*

Avoidant behavior: Say certain phrases over and over again so that nothing bad will happen.

Monkey logic: *Because you said those phrases, nothing bad happened to someone you love.*

Monkey thought: *What if your girlfriend got in a car accident and that's why she is late?*

Avoidant behavior: Call her to make sure she is okay.

Monkey logic: *Because you called her, she is okay.*

This is why avoidance, although an easy way to reduce your anxiety fast, is the worst long-term solution. Every time you avoid a situation, you are giving your monkey a banana, feeding monkey logic, encouraging your monkey to reuse the anxious thought and others like it again in the future. Before you know it you are trapped in an ever-stronger cycle of avoidance.

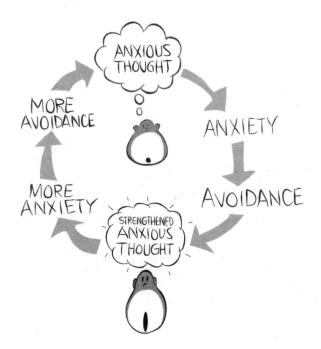

When Justin went to the skate park the next day, he noticed for the first time that the dogs in the nearby dog park were off-leash. The thought popped into his mind that someone might open the gate and one of the dogs that was off-leash could escape and attack him. He tried to keep skating, but he was so distracted by his new thought and the anxious feelings it brought up that he fell twice, and finally he called his dad to come pick him up.

More avoidance means more missing out on things that are important to you. Justin was missing out on the independence he had skateboarding all over town on his own. Depending on his parents to drive him places was unreliable because they were sometimes too busy. Worse yet was the frustration he felt at having to depend on them more when what he wanted was to depend on them less. And now he couldn't hang out with his friends at the skate park. Justin's world was getting smaller and smaller.

Is your world getting smaller? Are you not dating because of anxiety? Avoiding school? Maybe you can't go on camping trips or travel anywhere far from home. Are doctor and dentist visits something you avoid? Perhaps you believe that worrying will prevent bad things from happening. You may over-plan things, make too many lists, study too much, or procrastinate. Maybe you manage your anxiety with repeated washing or checking, or by saying and doing things in a certain way. Or maybe you use drugs or alcohol to avoid feeling anxious.

It is this *avoidance of anxiety* that is taking up so much time and energy that you have nothing left for what really matters to you. And as long as you keep feeding your monkey, that avoidance cycle will only get worse. Make no mistake about it: in order to reclaim your life, you need to stop the avoidance cycle in its tracks!

Chapter 3

Spot the Monkey

Identifying Anxious Thoughts

Reading this book thus far, you have been using a part of your brain that's totally different from the monkey mind. You've been using the rest of your brain, which sees the big picture and can take everything into account, not just potential threats. You are also listening to your heart. In your heart you know that there is more to your life than just staying alive. In your heart you hold your dreams of the future, how you want to live your life.

This whole book is based on the central idea that you are not your monkey. The better you get at seeing the difference between the real you and that frightened little critter, the better chance you have of taking back control of your life. You—and by that I mean the bigger, smarter you—will learn to "spot the monkey": to recognize monkey chatter and become aware of how it triggers your anxious feelings and avoidance.

Tools to Tame the Monkey Mind

Here are some great tools for spotting and taming that cute little beast. They will be worth every minute you spend on them.

Life Compass

Ask yourself whether you are moving *toward* things and situations you want to do and that are important to you. Or are you moving *away* from them? If you find yourself avoiding a situation that you really don't want to avoid, even though there is no immediate danger, it's likely your monkey had a hand in it.

Justin loved skateboarding and the independence it gave him, yet monkey chatter put him in his parents' car instead. Your monkey doesn't take into account how you want to live your life. Your monkey mind's only concern is keeping you alive.

Spot the Thought

Think of a situation that makes you anxious. Then ask yourself these three questions:

1. *What am I afraid of?*

2. *What's the worst that could happen if this comes true?*

3. *What would this mean about me, my life, or my future?*

These are the thoughts that drove your behavior in that situation. These thoughts might be reasonable and true— signals that this situation is somehow dangerous for you. Or they could be false alarms, a product of the monkey mind.

Let's follow along with Justin as he spots his thoughts.

1. What if that dog gets off its leash?

2. That dog might attack me.

3. I'm such a wimp, needing my parents to drive me!

Monkey Miscalculations

Compared to you, monkeys aren't very bright, and neither is the monkey mind. When determining risk, the monkey mind consistently makes two mistakes: it *over*estimates the threat of something bad happening, and it *under*estimates your ability to cope if something bad *were* to happen.

This double monkey miscalculation classifies safe situations as dangerous, setting off false alarms and putting your body into fight-or-flight mode. Overestimating or underestimating is just one way the monkey mind consistently miscalculates threats. Let's look at some of the other kinds of monkey miscalculations.

Catastrophizing

Leaping to the worst possible conclusion, or *catastrophizing*, is perhaps the most common monkey miscalculation. Like a scary movie, the monkey mind is always imagining the worst possible outcome. Here are some examples of catastrophizing thoughts:

- You're considering raising your hand to answer a question in class. *If you get this wrong, a rumor will start around school that you're stupid.*

- Your boyfriend hasn't returned a text. *He isn't answering your text; he must be breaking up with you.*

- While driving, you feel a bump. *Did you run somebody over?*

- You see a spider on the wall. *It could be poisonous. What if it jumps onto you and bites you?*

- Your chest feels tight. *Are you having a heart attack?*

- You are having difficulty on a test. *If you flunk this it will show up on your transcript and you won't get into college.*

If you think your monkey mind is catastrophizing, ask it, "What's really likely to happen?"

Discounting the Positive

Nearly every experience we have has good aspects and bad aspects, but the monkey mind, being obsessed with looking for threats and danger, completely ignores what is going well and focuses only on what is going poorly. We call this *discounting the positive*. Examples:

- While giving an oral presentation, you don't notice that most of the class is listening attentively. All you see is Janelle in the back, who is looking at her cell phone. *You are boring everyone!*

- You get an English paper back with an A-minus grade and several positive comments. Your eyes immediately go to the one suggestion for improvement. *You are hopeless at writing!*

- You invite a friend to the movies. He has other plans but he thanks you for the invitation. *He rejected you. You should never have dared to invite him!*

- You hear of a party you were not invited to. You don't know the host very well and you get invited to plenty of other parties, but your monkey says, *You're so unpopular!*

Ask your monkey, *What did I do that was okay?*

Labeling

Also known as part-whole thinking, labeling is applying a part of yourself to the whole of yourself. You may label yourself with harsh judgments you would never dare say to a friend but freely tell yourself. For example:

- You get a C on a quiz that you expected to do better on. *You're so stupid.*

- You miss a shot in a basketball game. *What an idiot! You should never shoot from this range.*

- You tell a joke that offends someone. *You are such a fool! You should keep your mouth shut!*

- You get beaten in a class election by a dozen votes. *You are such a loser!*

Ask yourself, *Does this label apply to me all the time in all situations?*

Mind Reading

The monkey mind is so sensitive to criticism that it imagines other people are thinking critical thoughts about you!

- You're walking down the hallway with a new hairdo. *Everybody is staring at your hair in horror!*

- You're eating alone at a sandwich shop. *It looks like you have no friends. The guys behind the counter think you're a loser!*

- A friend is checking her texts during your conversation. *She thinks you're boring!*

If you think your monkey is reading minds, ask yourself, *What evidence do I have that this is what people are actually thinking?*

Perfectionism

You must perform flawlessly, every time, all the time. Anything less isn't good enough and will leave you vulnerable to criticism and other danger. So says the monkey mind.

- You're looking at a supermodel in a magazine. *You need to lose five pounds so you can look like that.*

- After a ten-mile run, you realize you are fifteen seconds off yesterday's time. *You better do another mile. You don't deserve to rest.*

- You got an A in Biology, but your friend got an A-plus. *You should have gotten up early this morning to study!*

- During a presentation in English your voice shakes and you stumble on your words a few times. *That was unacceptable! And the whole class could see that you were anxious!*

- You just spent three hours on a take-home essay
  after the teacher said it shouldn't take longer than
  an hour. Even so, you don't feel like it is as good as
  it could or should be. And you still have your math
  and Spanish homework to do! *You need to take off
  school tomorrow so you can spend all day catching up.*

Not sure if you are a perfectionist? Ask yourself, *Am I
expecting more of myself than I would expect of someone else?*

Intolerance of Uncertainty

No matter how the odds favor a positive result, if there
is even a 1 percent chance that things could go wrong, the
monkey mind cannot rest.

- You hear a siren. *What if that's an ambulance taking
  your mom to the hospital?*

- You need to use a public toilet. *What if you can catch AIDS from a toilet seat?*

- You have a pain in your gut. *This could be stomach cancer.*

- Your friend just picked you up at your house. *What if you left the curling iron on and the house burns down?*

Ask yourself, *What is the cost I am paying to eliminate all risk from my life?*

Now let's take another look at Justin's anxious thoughts, this time looking for monkey miscalculations.

What if the dog gets off the leash?

That dog might attack me.

I am such a wimp, needing my parents to drive me!

Justin was *catastrophizing* by jumping to the conclusion that this dog might get off its leash and attack him. He was also *discounting the positive.* He did not consider that this was a dog he had skated by many times before and it had not shown any signs of aggression. Justin was *labeling* by calling himself a wimp. He took plenty of risks—in fact, he was one of the more daring of his friends when it came to skateboarding. Justin was probably *not tolerating uncertainty* either. He was unwilling to take the chance that other dogs would attack him.

Identifying the monkey miscalculations in your anxious thoughts helps you think more objectively. If the thought is inaccurate and there is no actual danger, then the anxiety that thought triggers is a false alarm. Knowing that allows you to distance yourself from your monkey, and it opens you up to new ideas and possibilities. What kinds of thoughts happen when you take *everything* into consideration, not just your monkey's wild guesses?

Alternative Thoughts

This tool is really the second half of the "Spot the Thought" exercise. Here you'll respond to the anxious thoughts you now know are monkey chatter with some new, alternative ideas. These *alternative thoughts* will lay the groundwork for a new way to think and ultimately a new way to live your life.

Here are some of Justin's *alternative thoughts*:

I have been around a lot of dogs and never actually been attacked.

Most dogs are on leashes.

Just because I feel afraid does not mean I'm in danger.

The possibility of a dog getting off its leash and attacking me is very unlikely.

Now Justin had a choice. He had two ways to think about the problem, and one offered a lot more hope than the other.

If you haven't already, try the Spot the Thought and Alternative Thoughts exercises for yourself. Think back to some situations that made you anxious this past week. Download the worksheets available at http://www .newharbinger.com/32431, or just grab a paper and pencil and get to work.

At this point your monkey mind is probably screeching in protest over all this close examination. It doesn't like you second-guessing its warnings of danger (even though they are wild guesses to begin with). It will be a struggle at first, but things will get better. After using these tools a few times on paper, you will be able to ask and answer these questions in your head whenever the need arises.

What we have learned so far about the monkey mind is that it is always chattering, and if we are not careful, it will automatically drive our feelings and behavior. When you pay attention to the chatter, you are rewarding the monkey. It loves attention. For the monkey, attention is as good as a banana. The problem is, the more you feed the monkey the more it will chatter.

Mindfulness Tools

Mindfulness practice is designed to help you take your attention away from your monkey mind. Mindfulness has been around for at least twenty-five hundred years and is used more and more in our modern world with great benefit. There are three basic parts to it, each of which can be helpful in spotting your monkey.

Focused Attention

As I've pointed out, it takes no effort to focus on the monkey mind's chatter. The chatter is so distracting and automatic that we don't even know we are being hijacked by our monkey mind. You can reduce the chatter and the effect it has on you by choosing where to place your attention.

You can focus on anything at all—a photo, a flower, a spot on the wall. What matters is that you are not giving the monkey the attention that it is used to. Many people find that the best place to focus their attention is on their own breath. Your lungs will always be there, and when you become aware of your breath you become aware of your body.

Focused attention on the breath is best done when sitting in a quiet place where there are no obvious distractions. Notice the air as it moves in and out of your nostrils, or notice your belly as it expands on the in-breath and deflates on the out-breath. Every time your monkey mind gets you thinking about something other than your breath, say, *Thank you, monkey.* Then gently bring your attention back to your breathing.

You will in all likelihood be distracted over and over again. Don't be discouraged by this. In fact, the more often you catch yourself being distracted by the monkey mind the better. The whole point of this practice is to notice these distractions and to choose to bring your attention back to your breath.

Present Moment

The monkey mind is constantly reviewing the past for mistakes you may have made. When it is not doing that, it is scanning the future for signs of danger. This of course creates anxiety. By focusing on the *present moment* we can get distance from all this chatter and actually experience relief. It also allows us to live more fully and realize that everything is in a constant state of change.

Right now you are reading this sentence. You may also be thinking that you're almost at the end of the chapter and wondering whether you should take a break or keep reading. Take a moment right now to just notice the feeling of the book in your hand. Notice where you are sitting or lying down. Become aware of the sounds in the room right now, or the silence. The simple act of noticing and paying attention to your immediate surroundings puts you in the present moment. The past and the future are the territory of the monkey mind. The present is yours and yours alone.

You can practice paying attention at any time—while brushing your teeth, taking a shower, or putting a spoonful of cereal in your mouth. If you are walking down the street, try really looking at the trees and buildings and people around you. If you are sitting somewhere, close your eyes and just listen. You'll be amazed at what you hear. More importantly, you will notice the thoughts that pop up, how random they are, and what a distraction they are from the moment you are in. You don't have to fight those thoughts; it's only your monkey doing its job a little too well. Just notice them and let them go.

When you begin to pay attention throughout your day, you will be amazed to discover all the monkey chatter that distracts you. Don't be discouraged. Thank your monkey and bring yourself back to being right here, right now.

Acceptance

As you get better at spotting monkey chatter, you'll recognize another theme besides the scary warnings of danger. You will notice judgments, both about yourself and about others. Your monkey may be telling you what you should or should not have done, that you are lazy or weak, or similar things about others. How helpful is this? Not helpful at all! Having ideas about how you *should* be will only make you discouraged. The first point I made in this book is that there is no normal and nobody is perfect. Everyone has a monkey, everyone has anxiety of some kind, and everyone certainly makes mistakes. You will be able to move forward only by accepting yourself *as you are*.

Accepting that anxiety is normal and that you are not to blame for it will enable you to have compassion for yourself. You've suffered enough without piling on judgments and blame. When you are compassionate with a friend who is down, what happens? The friend is encouraged. It works the same way on you. When you accept your anxiety and forgive yourself for having it, you unlock the most powerful tool of all: courage. When you can unleash your own courage on a problem, everything is possible!

> *Knowing that his fears about dogs were based on miscalculations gave Justin some hope. Maybe he didn't have to be so afraid of dogs. He also began practicing mindfulness throughout his day. When he noticed his mind wandering to thoughts about dogs, or anything else that seemed like the work of his monkey, he brought his attention back to the present moment. And he made real progress with some of the judgments he'd been making about himself—about being a wimp, for example. He was beginning to feel more confident about his future.*

One Saturday afternoon he grabbed his skateboard out of the closet and took off for the skate park. It felt amazing to be back out in the world, free and on his own. All his work was paying off. Everything was going great until a pickup truck passed him with a dog barking in the back.

Immediately Justin was hit with a wave of fear. He jumped off his skateboard and turned around for home. He just couldn't go any farther. As he trudged back he reviewed his alternative thoughts. The dog in the truck had been tied. He wasn't even sure it was barking at him. He knew in his head that there hadn't been any real danger, but in his body he felt really vulnerable. I need to get rid of this feeling, *he thought.* What else do I have to do to get over this stupid fear of dogs?

Chapter 4

Rule the Monkey

Take Back Control of Your Life

I f you've read this far and done the exercises, you are in a much better place than you were before. You can recognize your monkey chatter and how it triggers your anxiety. You have come up with some alternative thoughts, without all those monkey miscalculations in them, and that has probably helped reduce your anxiety a bit. You may even be beginning to tell the difference between real threats and false alarms. Congratulations!

At the same time, if you are still responding to monkey chatter by avoiding situations that make you anxious, then you are still feeding your monkey bananas and continuing the cycle of avoidance. To live the kind of life you want, to go where you need to go to accomplish your goals, you will have to begin to face situations and take actions that make you anxious.

If you are like most anxious teens, you've always thought, *Isn't my anxiety something I have to get rid of before I can do things?*

Even if you have already wised up to your monkey's miscalculations and developed alternative thoughts, for you to actually believe these situations are manageable you will have to experience them. You won't be able to do this if you continue to act as if anxiety is to be avoided.

In the past, you've allowed your monkey to run your life with its wild guesses and false alarms. Your monkey isn't to blame; it's just trying to do its job. But it has way too much power over you. You can't keep playing by your monkey's rules. You need to rule the monkey.

To take back control of your life you'll have to change your behavior as well as your thinking. Instead of avoiding the things that your monkey tells you are dangerous, you'll have to move *toward* them and be willing to feel the anxiety that goes with that. When you move toward your anxiety you reverse the cycle. Your monkey has no power over you. *Sorry little one—no banana!*

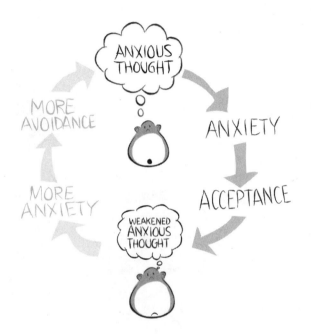

Right now there is probably a voice somewhere in the background sounding like, *Woo-woo-woo! Be very afraid!* It is true—to live the life you want you will have to start feeling the anxiety you've been avoiding. Is the life you want to live worth facing your fears?

Well, this is a question for you, not your monkey. It's too important a decision to base on a miscalculation. The answer to this question lies in your heart.

Tools to Rule the Monkey Mind

Here are a couple of tools to help you face your anxiety and take control of your life. Use either one, or both, to show that pesky monkey who's boss.

Life Compass

What are you missing out on because of anxiety? Dating? Travel? Social events? Are you spending big chunks of time worrying, rechecking things, or performing other rituals? Get out your life compass and ask yourself which direction you want to go. With your monkey in charge, you'll always be headed south, toward safety. Try finding your true north instead.

A great way to help yourself find your own true north is to write out all the things that you are missing out on by avoiding what makes you anxious. Here's what Justin came up with:

Skateboarding to school myself

Going to my friends' houses alone

Physical exercise

Hanging out at the skate park

Independence: getting around town by myself

Rush I feel when I'm on my board

Looking cool to my peers

Justin wrote down all the things he was missing out on because of his fear of dogs. There was the rush he felt riding his skateboard, and the fun of hanging out at the skate park with his friends. He also missed the physical exercise. But there was one thing he missed that really stood out. Justin really hated depending on his parents to drive him around. He wanted to feel free again, able to go anywhere, anytime he chose. Giving up his independence was a deal-breaker for Justin; he just couldn't see himself continuing to live that way. Independence was something he valued enough that he decided he would be willing to face some discomfort to have it.

Good decision. Meeting a challenge even though you are afraid—and surviving the experience—is how you really gain distance from, and power over, your monkey mind. Justin will prove to himself that his anxious thoughts are indeed miscalculations, that his anxiety is based on a false alarm, and that when faced with anxiety he can cope. He will feel the power of being in control of his own destiny.

How about you? What do you want that your anxiety is holding you back from? Grab a pencil and paper and make your own list. Or use the Life Compass form at http://www .newharbinger.com/32431.

Allowing ourselves to feel the anxiety that comes with going after what we want is a new idea for most of us. We've avoided feeling anxious so long that the very idea of accepting anxiety seems crazy, and the idea of actually feeling it sounds overwhelming. True, it won't be easy. Like anything worth doing, it will take practice. But like anything that's difficult, you can do it in small steps.

The Challenge Ladder

Picture a ladder with the life you want to live at the top. It will be your ladder and yours alone. It makes no difference whether your goal is to leave home and go to college or simply to leave the house without rechecking your backpack a half-dozen times. The point is to go in *your* direction, not your monkey's.

On each rung you will place a challenge for yourself, each one slightly bigger and scarier than the one below it. As you meet each challenge you will become more powerful and more skilled at accepting anxiety as just a feeling, rather than something that should hold you back from going where you want to go.

Let's look at how Justin constructed his challenge ladder. It was important that his first rung be challenging enough to set off his monkey alarms, but not so challenging that he wouldn't be willing to do it.

Justin had a friend who had a dog named Charlie. Charlie was a small dog, and Justin guessed that if he were on a leash, he could handle hanging out with him for five minutes. It sounded easy, but Justin could tell from the anxiety he felt thinking about it that it would probably be more difficult than it sounded. And anyway, the point was not to make a dramatic leap but rather take a first step. Small challenges are what we learn from and are just as important as the bigger challenges on the higher rungs, because they prepare us for them.

Once Justin had that starting point, it wasn't too difficult to imagine slightly scarier challenges for the next rungs— like petting Charlie, or taking him off his leash. As he added more anxiety-provoking variables to each challenge, he found he was getting closer to his ultimate goal—on paper, at least. When he was finished, his ladder looked like this:

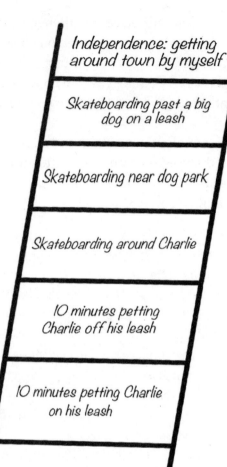

Independence: getting around town by myself

Skateboarding past a big dog on a leash

Skateboarding near dog park

Skateboarding around Charlie

10 minutes petting Charlie off his leash

10 minutes petting Charlie on his leash

5 minutes petting Charlie on his leash

Each rung had a challenge that would cause him a little more anxiety—and give him a little more independence—than the rung below it. Completing each challenge would help Justin gain a little more distance from his monkey's chatter and a little more confidence in his own alternative thought: *The possibility of a dog getting off its leash and attacking me is very unlikely.*

Every anxiety type has its own kinds of challenges, so hold off on making a ladder of your own until you've read the chapters that relate most to you. (In chapter 6, for example, I will go into more detail about specific phobias like Justin's.) For now, let's follow along with Justin as he takes his first tentative step.

> *It will come as no surprise that Justin's monkey didn't like the challenge ladder and was quite vocal about it.* Are you crazy? Woo-woo! Small dogs bite, too! *As Justin approached his friend's house he could hear Charlie barking inside.* He's probably barking at me, *Justin thought, breaking into a cold sweat.*

Wait a minute! It all looks great on paper, but how will Justin actually meet the challenges? Are we forgetting that he's absolutely terrified of dogs?

Chapter 5

Thank You, Monkey!

How Acceptance Sets You Free

Have you ever hiked up the side of a mountain? On a steep trail you get tired very quickly. It isn't long before you are sweaty and exhausted. The trail zigzags, and at each sharp turn a new stretch of challenging terrain appears. The trees keep you from seeing what lies ahead, and you wonder whether you will ever make it to the top. Turning back is so tempting. Your fatigue gets worse and worse until you can barely put one foot in front of the other, and then…

You reach the top! And like the trail, your fatigue levels off. Your legs are shaky and your body feels spent, but you also feel really good. You conquered the mountain.

Anxiety is like fatigue. As with choosing to climb a mountain, if you choose to face your fear it will get worse before it gets better. But remember, you don't hike up the mountain saying, *I shouldn't be tired! Being tired is unacceptable!* If you thought that, you would certainly turn around and head back to the bottom. You know that feeling tired is normal when climbing a steep trail, so you accept it. You know and trust that your fatigue will not kill you, and that if you rest at each bend and catch your breath, you will find the strength to reach your goal. Like fatigue, anxiety is much more tolerable if you accept it as a normal part of life.

Each rung of your challenge ladder is like a zigzag on that trail up the mountain. As you look at the new terrain, your success depends on your ability to welcome what it has to offer. On the trail, that includes the exhaustion in your body. On your ladder, it includes the anxiety you'll feel. When that anxiety comes, you will welcome it. You'll say, *Thank you, monkey! Can I have some more?*

The Welcoming Breath

Deciding to welcome anxiety won't be enough. You'll have to welcome it with your whole body, in the places where you feel the anxiety. In the past, when you've felt anxious you've breathed rapidly and shallowly, which is a fight-or-flight response. When you are welcoming anxiety you do the opposite:

1. Breathe in deeply, filling your lungs so that your belly expands.

2. Breathe out completely.

3. Repeat slowly and deliberately.

Not very complicated, is it? It may be simple, but it is also simply powerful. With each inhalation, imagine you are pulling strength from the ground like the roots of a tree. With each exhalation you are letting go of controlling the situation, bending like a tree in the wind, accepting whatever happens—including the anxiety it may bring.

Breathing into fear counters and softens your body's fight-or-flight sensations. Your monkey's howls of alarm tell your body to breathe shallowly and rapidly, but with your deep, slow breaths you override that command. With each breath you are saying, *I can handle this!*

A word of caution here: Don't try to relax. Don't picture yourself on a peaceful beach or a similar restful spot until your anxiety goes away. That's avoiding the situation. When you try to relax you are, in effect, giving your monkey a banana, rewarding its miscalculation, because you are agreeing with it that you couldn't handle feeling the anxiety. For your challenges to be successful and help you reach your goal, you will have to be fully present in the situation, just like in the mindfulness practice, feeling every moment completely.

As you accept your anxious feelings with your breath, if you happen to become relaxed, that is fine—just as fine as if you become more anxious. As long as you are welcoming your anxiety, breathing into your fear, you are meeting the challenge and climbing the ladder.

The End of Anxiety

This is a difficult idea to trust. Chances are you've never actually felt your anxiety all the way through. But the fact is, like everything in the natural world, anxiety has a beginning, a middle, and an end.

Try an experiment right now: Picture a situation, image, or thought that makes you anxious. Once you have that feeling in your body, breathe into it, allowing it to be exactly as it is, not trying to change anything. If you feel any tension in your body, breathe into that area. Continue to do this for five minutes, paying close attention to the sensations in your body.

You will notice the anxious feeling changing. It may grow more intense or less intense. It may move around your body. All of this is fine. By breathing into your anxiety you are decreasing your resistance to it and allowing it to run its natural course. What may surprise you is how well your body can process a bad feeling. You won't fall apart or faint or have a heart attack. You are much stronger than your monkey thinks you are!

Of course it won't be easy. Your monkey mind will be chattering away like always. Its false alarms will rise in volume until they drown out everything else. To tame your monkey you must move forward with a sense of purpose and authority, dragging the howling little critter along behind you.

Remember, you cannot reason, argue, or make deals with a monkey! All that does is give your monkey a chance to repeat all its danger warnings, cast doubt, and remind you how terrible it would be if you were wrong. Giving your monkey any attention at all is giving it opportunities to distract you from your commitment to yourself, which is to be in the situation and welcome anxiety. Just say, *Thank you, monkey!* and move forward.

> *As Justin approached his first challenge with Charlie, he felt all the feelings he knew he would. Lots of anxious thoughts about being bitten ran through his head and he felt a powerful urge to run. But by breathing slowly and deeply, and reminding himself about his ultimate goal of independence, he was able to open the gate, walk up the stairs, and ring the doorbell. A few seconds later he was standing in place next to a dog!*
>
> *Though his anxiety was very high at first, within a few minutes—to his surprise—it began to inch down a little. The longer he was near Charlie, and Charlie was not attacking him, the more he calmed down. He forgot about his fear of getting bitten, and all his monkey chatter faded into the background. Justin felt so relaxed that when Charlie put his paws up on his knee, he reached down instinctively to scratch Charlie's head.*

One small step for Justin, one large step toward Justin's independence! The whole way home he felt like he was walking on a cloud. In fact, a little part of Justin actually started looking forward to the next challenge. What was happening here?

As I pointed out in chapter 4, every time you avoid a situation you train your monkey to believe that its wild guesses about the dangers of that situation are correct. After years of avoidance you'll have a gorilla-size problem that seems beyond control. But the good news is that no matter how entrenched you are in a cycle of avoidance, you can turn things around. With acceptance and courage you will become strong enough to see the beast for what it is: a scared little monkey.

Why do I sound so confident? Because the same dynamic that grew the monkey will shrink it. When you survive a situation you've previously avoided, your monkey mind cannot claim credit. It gets no banana! You survived because the situation turned out to be manageable after all. Although it was scary, you survived, and this is how you gain confidence in your ability to tolerate anxiety and do what you want and need to do.

As you learn to accept anxiety as just a feeling, and not necessarily a sign that something is wrong, the chatter of your monkey mind will seem less compelling. Thoughts that once filled your head, like *I feel anxious; I'd better get out of here*, will be replaced by *I can be in this situation even though I am anxious*. Imagine all the things you will do, the places you will go, by patiently climbing your ladder one step at a time. I promise you that your life will improve once you calm the little critter down and learn not to take it so seriously!

Justin worked hard at climbing his ladder one rung at a time. With each challenge he felt another wave of anxiety, but he rode it out, letting his monkey howl away in the background. After a few rungs his alternative thought that dogs don't attack very often became stronger and more believable to him. Climbing his challenge ladder and practicing mindfulness made it easier and easier to ignore his monkey.

Soon he was back to skating to friends' houses and going to the skate park, almost as comfortably as he had before, and not needing to depend on his parents to get around. If he saw a large dog, he'd notice his heart beating faster, and his monkey mind would send out a warning thought like Uh-oh, that dog looks dangerous! *But he was able to say* Thank you, monkey! *and feel the anxiety without going back to avoidance. It wasn't long before Justin was taking his independence for granted.*

One day at the skate park another skater said, "Hey, you were gone for a while. You hurt yourself or something?"

"No," Justin answered. "I just took a break." Then, to himself, he added, —to tame a monkey! *He laughed and launched himself into the bowl.*

I hope that reading Justin's story will help you see your own anxiety in a different light. Are you ready to take back your life? The next six chapters, one or more of which will feel specially written for you, will zero in on specific types of anxiety. Have courage and know that you are not alone. Thousands of other teens have changed their lives this way. You can master your anxiety!

Part 2

Chapter 6

Shyness and Social Anxiety

Why Is Everyone Looking at Me?

Jarod had always been confident and outgoing until ninth grade, when he started to feel self-conscious and shy. One day he was telling a joke to a group of friends and one of them took offense, saying the joke was racist. Jarod felt humiliated and ashamed. After that he started giving more thought to what he was going to say before he said it. He wanted to make certain he would not offend anyone in normal conversations. Because he needed to plan every word he spoke he fell behind in conversations, becoming more and more quiet. By the time he was in high school the only way he felt he could be himself was if he drank alcohol at parties. But even then he often woke up the next day thinking about things he had said or how he had acted the night before, always with the same sense of shame.

J arod has social anxiety—the fear of doing or saying something that would cause others to ridicule or reject him, resulting in feelings of embarrassment, humiliation, and shame. Social anxiety is the most common type of anxiety, affecting one in twenty teens and adults. Many teens with social anxiety have been shy their whole lives; others, like Jarod, were outgoing as children but became shy or socially anxious during middle school or high school.

Here is a list of common situations that make many teens particularly anxious. Can you relate to any of them?

Starting or maintaining conversations

Answering questions in class

Asking someone on a date

Asking a teacher a question or for help

Attending parties, dances, or other social activities

Blushing, shaking, sweating, or showing other signs of anxiety

Eating or writing in front of others

Participating in P. E.

Inviting a friend to get together

Giving a report or reading in front of the class

Performing in front of others

Using school or public bathrooms

The Need to Belong

All throughout history, humans have been pack animals. We hunted in hunting parties, gathered nuts and berries in groups, and traveled in tribes or families. We had a much better chance of having something to eat and staying warm and safe when in a pack. In fact, an individual could not survive long alone in the wild. Naturally our ancestors learned to behave in ways that would not get them kicked out of their pack.

Modern-day teens want to fit in also. If you're rejected by your peers, you won't be eaten by wolves, starve, or freeze to death, but there will still be a cost to pay. Community and personal connections are essential to happiness and well-being. So a little anxiety is adaptive. You are more likely to thrive if you feel some concern when you mess up socially—enough to learn from, anyway.

But what if, like Jarod, you are afraid of "messing up" *all the time*? What if you feel as though every move you make is being judged, every word you utter is being ridiculed—as if everywhere you go you are on stage, in a spotlight performing for a highly critical audience? Social anxiety can cripple you at school, at your job, and in your social life.

The anxiety you feel is a normal fight-or-flight response. Your nervous system is doing exactly what it was designed to do, what it does for all threats to your safety. Except for one thing: you aren't in any danger. There is a monkey sounding the alarm.

It is your monkey mind's job to keep you safe, and from the monkey point of view, it would be dangerous for you if your peers disapproved of you. If you are reading this chapter and you identify with Jarod, chances are you have a monkey mind that is working overtime. When you are in a conversation your monkey is carefully monitoring everything you say, listening for anything that might sound weird to others. It is constantly scanning people's faces for signs of boredom or disapproval. Anything less than total approval is interpreted as a threat. In the monkey mind, if one person is bored by one thing you say, that could mean everyone will be bored by everything you say.

As we have learned, monkeys are not good at assessing risk. Monkey mind predictions are more like wild guesses than anything else. In your case, your monkey is making the universal over/under miscalculation:

1. It overestimates the threat that people will judge you to the extent that you become an outcast.

2. It underestimates your ability to cope if someone did negatively judge you.

With every monkey mind miscalculation another anxious thought pops into your head. These are the thoughts that prompt the behavior that all anxiety disorders share: avoidance. It is only natural to avoid situations that make you anxious, but when you do so you train your monkey mind to believe that its wild guesses about imaginary threats are correct, and you encourage it to make more of them. Your avoidant behavior is like feeding your monkey a banana. You just make it bigger and stronger and its false alarms harder to ignore.

Let's take a look at how Jarod's avoidance fed his monkey mind. Jarod's most anxious thought was *What if I say something offensive or stupid?* and his behavior was designed to avoid doing so at all costs. In conversations with his peers he kept quiet, avoiding his friends' possible judgments. If he really felt like he had something he needed to say, he avoided making any mistakes by rehearsing word-for-word first. Avoiding spontaneity kept Jarod out of trouble, and his monkey mind claimed credit. Jarod's monkey logic went like this: *Because you didn't say anything, or you thought hard about exactly what to say first, you did not insult anyone or say something that would have made people dislike you.*

At parties Jarod was able to loosen up and ignore his monkey more easily by drinking alcohol. But this caused problems, too. And the next day his monkey was right back at it, fretting over things he said or did while drunk. And he felt even more uncomfortable around people that he had met at the party because he was back to being quiet and withdrawn. He worried they would expect him to be more fun and outgoing, like he was when he had been drinking.

Jarod was trapped in a cycle of avoidance. The more he avoided speaking spontaneously the more he encouraged his monkey to set off alarms about the dangers of social situations in which he might have to speak. By using alcohol to cover up his anxiety he avoided gaining confidence in speaking more spontaneously without it. Jarod's world was getting smaller and smaller, and he wasn't happy about it.

Tools to Tame the Social Anxiety Monkey

As you know, you cannot simply get rid of your anxious thoughts. Your monkey mind is a built-in safety feature and it is here to stay. But that doesn't mean you have to accept your monkey's judgment of everything going on around you. You can question monkey thoughts and begin to interrupt your cycle of avoidance. To question those thoughts you have to know what they are. You have to spot your monkey.

Spot the Thought

When monkey-spotting, good questions to ask yourself are: *What am I afraid of? What would this mean about me? What would others think of me? What is the worst that could happen if this were true?*

Jarod picked a situation that provokes anxiety for many teens—wanting to talk to the girl next to him in class. Here are his answers to those three questions:

> I won't be able to think what to say!
>
> I'll say something strange and she'll think I'm weird!
>
> She'll tell all her friends how weird I am and no one will like me!

To help you spot your thoughts, download the Spot the Thought for Social Anxiety worksheet available at http://www.newharbinger.com/32431.

Monkey Miscalculations

Although monkey chatter may feel true and accurate, it is made up of more wild guesses than facts. The most common kinds of miscalculations that occur with social anxiety are the following:

Mind Reading

The monkey mind is so sensitive to criticism that it imagines other people are thinking critical thoughts about you! For example:

- *He thinks you are boring.*

- *She thinks you sound like a fraud.*

- *They think you're a loser.*

- *She thinks you were showing off.*

- *They notice you are nervous and they think you are weird and weak.*

If your monkey is mind reading, ask yourself, *What evidence do I have that this is what people are thinking about me?* Asking and answering this question can help you disengage from the monkey's chatter and get a better perspective.

Catastrophizing

Rather than considering all possible outcomes, your monkey takes a giant leap to the worst thing that could possibly happen. For example:

- *If people notice you are nervous they will tell others and everyone will think you're weird.*

- *People will point at you or laugh at you.*

- *You'll freeze up and not be able to think of something to say in a conversation.*

- *If you have to give an oral presentation you may faint or pass out.*

Ask yourself, *What is most likely to happen? How could I cope with that?*

Perfectionism

You must perform flawlessly, every time, all the time. Anything less isn't good enough and will leave you vulnerable to criticism and serious rejection. For example:

- *You must avoid stumbling over a word or else people will think you are nervous.*

- *You should never answer a question wrong in class or else people will think you are stupid.*

- *You need to always know what to say or else people will think you are awkward.*

- *You should always remember people's names or else people will think you are insensitive or don't care about them.*

- *You must look calm, confident, and relaxed, or else people will think you are weird.*

- *You should always be interesting or else people will think you are boring.*

Ask yourself, *Am I expecting more of myself than I would of others?*

Labeling

Your monkey looks at one part of what you might say or do and decides that it defines you as a person. Labels can be harsh judgments you freely use on yourself but would never dream of saying to a friend. For example:

- You asked a dumb question. *You are such an idiot!*

- You forgot someone's name. *You are such a dope!*

- You sweated right through your shirt. *You are so disgusting!*

- You could not think of what to say. *You are so dumb!*

- That was awkward. *You are so weird!*

If you think your monkey is labeling, ask yourself, *Does this word apply to me all the time, in every situation?*

Intolerance of Uncertainty

Since you never really know what others are thinking, there is always lots of room for uncertainty. But if there is even a 1 percent chance that someone might judge you, your monkey concludes *It's not worth it.*

- *What if you say something offensive?*

- *What if someone laughs at you?*

- *What if someone notices you are sweaty and thinks you are gross?*

If your monkey mind is making this miscalculation you can ask yourself, *Is it always better to be safe than sorry?* By never taking any chances you are guaranteeing that you will never get what you want.

Alternative Thoughts

Identifying the miscalculations in these thoughts helps you see the difference between you and your monkey mind. Assessing risk is too important a job to leave to that primitive part of your brain. Stepping back from your monkey chatter opens up space for new ways of thinking.

Jarod had been listening to his monkey mind since junior high, and it was hard for him to believe there was any other way to think. But once he began questioning it, he was able to come up with his own alternative thoughts.

Monkey thought: *If you pause in the conversation or stumble on a word she will think you are stupid.*

Jarod's alternative thought: *That's mind reading! I have no way of knowing what she will think.*

Monkey thought: *She will tell all her friends how weird you are.*

Jarod's alternative thought: *That's catastrophizing. I would have to say something really strange for it to be worthy of gossip, and that's unlikely.*

Monkey thought: *To initiate a conversation, you'd have to say something interesting.*

Jarod's alternative thought: *I don't have to be perfect. If someone started a conversation with me, I would like that and would not be concerned about whether the person sounded interesting or not.*

Monkey thought: *You may say something offensive; it's not worth the risk.*

Jarod's alternative thought: *If I don't say anything at all I have no chance of getting to know her, so it is worth the risk.*

Alternative thoughts give you something else to focus on besides your monkey's chatter. When you focus on your alternative thoughts you deny your monkey the attention it is used to. This is the first step toward taming your monkey.

You can download an Alternative Thoughts worksheet at http://www.newharbinger.com/32431.

Tools to Rule the Social Anxiety Monkey

Jarod felt very encouraged by his alternative thoughts. When he thought about being spontaneous with other people— saying what he was thinking without planning every word— he felt that he could do it. He decided to test his new attitude the next day at school and see what happened.

Spotting your monkey and having alternative thoughts to replace your anxious ones can give you courage to approach situations that you have been avoiding. But once you are in those situations you are still going to get false alarms from your monkey that make you feel anxious.

To rule the monkey mind you will have to learn how to tolerate anxiety. You will have to be willing to actually feel it. When you can stay in a situation even though it makes you feel anxious, you will stop the cycle of anxiety. You just have to play by your own rules—not your monkey's!

Life Compass

Facing situations that you've been avoiding will take courage. To unleash your full power you will need an inspiring goal, one important to you that you will keep moving forward despite the discomfort of feeling anxious and the sound of your monkey's howls.

Your goal could be mastering a specific situation, like going to your senior prom; or it could be a human value, like being authentic in your interactions with others. That is up to you.

Jarod made a list of things that were important to him that he was missing out on.

1. Starting or joining conversations

2. Asking someone out on a date (without being drunk)

3. Saying what I really think

4. Feeling comfortable with my friends

These things were Jarod's true north on his compass, and he was determined not to let his monkey point him south.

You can download a Life Compass worksheet at http://www.newharbinger.com/32431.

The Challenge Ladder

Whatever your goal is, you can reach it if you approach it one step at a time. Picture your goal at the top of a ladder. Each rung of the ladder will be a specific challenge designed by you to bring you closer to your goal.

When Jarod asked himself what he wanted at the top of his ladder, the answer was clear: he wanted to be spontaneous with people, to be able to say what he was thinking and feeling. There were two specific situations he'd been avoiding because he'd been afraid to do just that, and they were important enough to him that he was ready to fight for them.

Jarod thought he would begin working on starting or joining conversations because he figured if he could do this, it would also help him move up to asking someone on a date. He decided that his first ladder would be totally devoted to starting or joining conversations.

Making a ladder for yourself can be tricky because there are so many variables. For social anxiety you can reduce them to three W's: who, what, and where.

Start with the following question: Who are the people you've been avoiding? Rate each one for scariness. Then, come up with a few options for what you might do with the people you've listed, and where. Rate the scariness of these options too. The "Who, What, Where" list Jarod made looked like this:

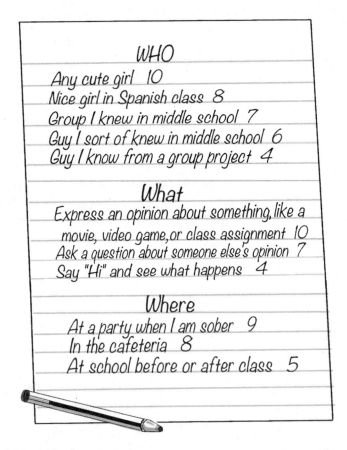

WHO

Any cute girl 10
Nice girl in Spanish class 8
Group I knew in middle school 7
Guy I sort of knew in middle school 6
Guy I know from a group project 4

What

Express an opinion about something, like a
   movie, video game, or class assignment 10
Ask a question about someone else's opinion 7
Say "Hi" and see what happens 4

Where

At a party when I am sober 9
In the cafeteria 8
At school before or after class 5

By looking at all three variables, Jarod was able to construct a ladder that started off with something a little bit scary and built toward something that would be really scary—

and rewarding! The bottom rung was simply *"(what)* Saying 'hi' to *(who)* a guy I know from a group project *(where)* before class."

Each challenge he set for himself on the rungs above it was a little scarier than the one just below it, but would bring him closer to his goal. The top rung was *"(what)* Asking a question of *(who)* a cute girl *(where)* at a party while sober."

You can download a Who, What, Where worksheet of your own at http://www.newharbinger.com/32431.

Jarod's Ladder

You may be wondering why Jarod went to all this trouble planning these situations. Wouldn't opportunities like these come up on their own soon enough? Yes, and when they did Jarod's monkey would sound the alarm and put him in fight-or-flight mode before Jarod had a chance to interpret the situation correctly.

You are better off surprising your monkey than letting it surprise you. Don't wait for the challenge. Seek it out and welcome it!

You can download a Challenge Ladder worksheet at http://www .newharbinger.com/32431.

Ladder
Ask a cute girl a question at a party while sober
Express an opinion to the nice girl in my Spanish class
Express an opinion in a group in the cafeteria
Ask someone's opinion while with a group of guys
Say hi to a guy I knew in middle school
Smile at a guy I know from a group project before class

Focused Attention

When you are in a situation that makes you feel anxious, monkey chatter grabs a lot of your attention. You are also hyperaware of the sensations in your body, like your heartbeat, sweating or blushing, or queasiness. If you put all of your attention on these things it amplifies their effect.

Focused attention is a mindfulness practice that can help you stay centered and grounded in even the scariest situations.

By choosing to focus on things outside your body you can reduce the anxious sensations you are feeling inside it. By choosing to focus on other people you take the spotlight off yourself.

When Jarod was having a conversation with a girl, instead of focusing on what his monkey was telling him and how anxious he felt, he focused on her. He listened extra carefully to what she was saying. He paid special notice to the color of her hair and her eyes and to what she was wearing. He was surprised at how much more relaxed the conversation was when he focused on her, and it seemed to him that she appreciated the attention, too.

To get good at focusing your attention away from your monkey mind, daily practice is important. When you're learning this skill, it is best to start by practicing when you are not anxious. As you get better at it, you can use it in situations like conversations and oral presentations—any challenge you have on your ladder.

The Problem with Perfect

Your monkey will also try to trick you into expecting perfect outcomes to your challenges and judging them accordingly. Remember that you are setting goals that you can accomplish, but they're challenging because they make you anxious. That means things will not go perfectly.

How would Jarod judge his performance on the first rung of his ladder—saying "Hi" and seeing what happens with the guy he knew from a group project—if his expectations were to sound calm and confident and have no awkward silences? If he has perfectionistic expectations he will almost certainly fail and wind up feeling pretty bad about himself.

Set a Realistic Goal

A more realistic goal for Jarod would be to smile and say "Hi"—*period*. If the other boy responded and a conversation started, great! If not, or if Jarod blushed, sweated, or stumbled over his words, it wouldn't matter.

Jarod met his first-rung challenge, but afterward he started to worry about how he had sounded. He also noticed feeling hot and wondered if the other boy had seen that he was nervous. Then he realized that this was his monkey chattering away at him. Once he spotted his monkey he was able to remind himself that he had accomplished his realistic goal, and he felt really good about himself. Learning to praise yourself for what you are doing right and being realistic about what to expect of yourself are both essential for overcoming social anxiety.

As long as you meet your original challenge, you win. You've interrupted the cycle of avoidance. Your monkey gets no banana and it's a little tamer than before. And most important, you are playing by *your* rules, not your monkey's.

You can download a Realistic Goal worksheet at http://www.newharbinger.com/32431.

Rolling with It

Remember the other half of the over/under monkey miscalculation? It underestimates your ability to cope if something bad happens. Well, it is important to remember that not everyone is going to respond positively to you. Sometimes you will be ignored or even criticized. This is what triggered Jarod's social anxiety in the first place—his friend telling him his joke was racist.

You know what skateboarders say: "If you're not falling, you're not skating." Even the best basketball players miss their shots more than half the time. Sometimes they miss ten shots in a row. Whether you are skateboarding, shooting hoops, or hanging out with friends, you are going to have awkward moments in which you look less than perfect.

Acceptance

The fact is, everybody makes mistakes. If you put yourself in a challenging situation and somebody reacts negatively to you, your monkey mind is going to sound a full-scale alarm, hit you with a deluge of anxious thoughts, and shower you with shame. This is the time to take care of yourself, not punish yourself. How do we take care of ourselves? With a very simple three-step process:

1. Take a deep breath deep down into your belly.

2. Slowly exhale.

3. Repeat.

Remember that when others are judgmental or harsh with you, it says more about them than you. You know for a fact that you are a decent person and that your intentions are good. If they have a problem respecting you, it is their problem, not yours, and you are wasting time and energy trying to impress them. Whatever the outcome of your challenge, you can take care of yourself.

If Jarod had been able to do this when he told that joke, he might have avoided a boatload of pain. He might have had an alternative thought like, *Oops, I goofed. I did not mean to be racist, but I can see how that joke could be taken that way, and then said to his friend that he was sorry.* This would have allowed him to move on. But he couldn't do that because he was being ruled by his monkey mind, which was operating under the assumption that mistakes meant getting kicked out of the tribe. Not anymore!

Jarod spotted his monkey and he knew now where it would lead him. He was determined to achieve his goal of being spontaneous and speaking his mind, and he was willing to accept the risk that he might embarrass himself in the process. As he met each challenge on his ladder he was delighted to discover that people mostly responded well to him. When they didn't, he took some breaths and gave himself a pat on the back—although he didn't get the response he would have liked, he did meet the challenge and he wasn't avoiding anymore!

Over the next six months Jarod slowly worked his way up the rungs of his ladder, all the way to the top. His final challenge was a great success, even though the girl declined to go out with him. It might have been because she was going with someone else, or that he wasn't her type—Jarod didn't ask. He took a breath and rolled with it, and they wound up talking for about twenty minutes about their favorite bands. They are friends now, and Jarod is working on a new ladder. He's got big plans for the future.

The truth is, if you are a socially anxious teen, you are an intelligent, sensitive, and responsible person. Your biggest critic is inside you, not outside. You deserve to rule. Tell your monkey thank you, but it's miscalculated again. You aren't in any great danger, and whatever happens, you can cope!

Chapter 7

Panic and Agoraphobia

Am I Dying or Going Crazy?

Kim was sitting in the stands at her boyfriend's football game when she suddenly had a tight feeling in her chest, as if someone were squeezing her really hard. She had trouble catching her breath, her heart seemed like it was beating out of her chest, and she felt light-headed and dizzy. She called her parents, who came and picked her up and took her to the emergency room. The doctor told her that she was having a panic attack and that, other than that, there was nothing wrong with her.

If you've ever had a panic attack, you know how difficult it is to believe that there is nothing wrong with you. Suddenly, out of the blue and without warning, you feel like you are suffocating, or having a heart attack, or going crazy—or even all of those at the same time. Yet *nothing is wrong?*

Well, something *is* wrong, but it's not with your body. It's your monkey mind at work, setting off alarms when there is no physical danger. When Kim's chest tightened up and her heart rate increased—uncomfortable sensations for her—her monkey decided something was wrong. This is how a panic attack works, in slow motion:

Kim was relieved to be told that nothing was wrong with her, and by the time she left the ER she felt almost normal. Things were fine until about three weeks later, when she had another panic attack while sitting in her biology class. She remembered what the ER doctor had said, but unfortunately, knowing that nothing was wrong "physically" did not help her feel less anxious. She was so light-headed that she was afraid she would faint or lose control in some way. She managed to stand up and leave the classroom, telling her teacher she felt ill. Then she called her mother to come pick her up right away. Her mother made an appointment with Kim's doctor the next day to see if there was anything they could do. The doctor prescribed medication for Kim to take if she had another panic attack.

After the second panic attack Kim began to worry that she would have another one. She carried her pills with her at all times, as well as her cell phone, in case she needed to call her parents. She began to watch for signs of panic. Whenever she felt an increase in her heart rate she worried that she would have another attack, and sometimes she did. Kim took a pill as soon as she felt the sensations coming on, and this usually kept her from having a full-blown panic attack.

No matter how much you want to believe that panic attacks are not dangerous, they are so intense, so scary, that the thought of having another one causes you great anxiety. The monkey mind doesn't learn from reading facts or listening to emergency room doctors.

After the second attack, Kim's monkey concluded that because her "dangerous" physical symptoms went away shortly after her mother arrived, leaving the classroom and calling her mother stopped the attack. When Kim takes medicine to dull her panic, and it reduces her symptoms, her monkey says, *Medicine is good!* and sounds the alarm if she goes anywhere without her prescription bottle. As with all anxiety, the central characteristic of Kim's dilemma was her *avoidance*.

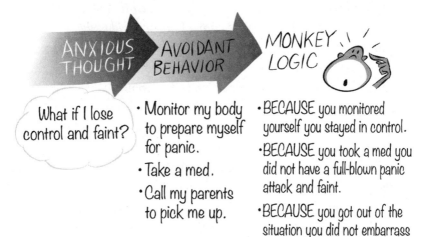

ANXIOUS THOUGHT	AVOIDANT BEHAVIOR	MONKEY LOGIC
What if I lose control and faint?	• Monitor my body to prepare myself for panic. • Take a med. • Call my parents to pick me up.	• BECAUSE you monitored yourself you stayed in control. • BECAUSE you took a med you did not have a full-blown panic attack and faint. • BECAUSE you got out of the situation you did not embarrass yourself by losing control.

And of course, avoidance does work. It became Kim's default behavior because it gave her a sense of control. Here are some common avoidance strategies used by teens who have panic disorder:

- Avoid exercise that makes you feel hot and sweaty or makes your heart beat fast.

- Avoid caffeine, which might make your heart beat fast or make you feel tense or jittery.

- Avoid any substance that might make you feel different. This could be over-the-counter medications, prescription medications, illegal drugs, or alcohol.

- Avoid hot and stuffy places like cars and classrooms because they make you feel hot and sweaty.

- Avoid any place where you have had a panic attack before.

- Avoid going anywhere without the medication that has been prescribed to you.

- Avoid going places without your cell phone, in case you feel panic coming on and feel you need to make an emergency call.

- Avoid going places without people who make you feel safe.

- Avoid going too far from home or hospitals.

The problem with all of these avoidance strategies is that they are dictated by anxious thoughts. When decisions are based on fear, your monkey mind is in control. The joy in life gets shoved aside because your monkey's only concern is keeping you safe. And while you may experience some sense of control, which decreases your anxiety in the short run, in the long run you are making your anxiety worse.

With every avoidance you strengthen your monkey's logic that your avoidance is what saved you. So your monkey's scary chatter gets louder and it seems more urgent. The relationship between your monkey's false alarms, your anxious feelings, and your avoidant behavior is reinforced. As more and more situations and activities are avoided, you wander farther from your goal.

Spotting the Panic Monkey

When Kim's monkey observed her her tight chest and racing heart, it sounded the alarm to *Woo-woo-woo! Get help! Be very afraid!* It was only trying to do its job of keeping Kim safe, but as we know, monkeys are not very good at assessing risks. Kim's monkey overestimated the physical danger of panic sensations, and it underestimated Kim's ability to cope with them.

So how physically dangerous are panic sensations? The fact is they are not dangerous at all. They are simply fight-or-flight reactions, evidence of your body's health more than anything. Here is a list of common panic attack symptoms, each with a classic misinterpretation as well as an explanation of what is really going on:

Sensation: Dizziness, light-headedness

Monkey thought: *What if you faint?*

Actual cause and purpose: Anxiety causes changes in your breathing so that you take in more oxygen and breathe out more carbon dioxide. This mix helps fuel the large muscles so that you can outrun or fight a threat. It also makes you dizzy and light-headed—but it doesn't make you faint! In order to actually faint, you need a sudden drop in your blood pressure. During a panic attack the opposite happens: your heart rate and blood pressure go up. So although this is a common fear, fainting is very unlikely to occur.

Sensation: Increased heart rate, heart palpitations, tightness in chest

Monkey thought: *What if you are having a heart attack?*

Actual cause and purpose: Your heart rate increases so that your heart can pump more oxygenated blood to your large muscles, letting you outrun or fight a threat. Your heart is a powerful muscle doing its job.

Sensation: Difficulty breathing

Monkey thought: *What if you suffocate and die?*

Actual cause and purpose: Your breathing becomes more rapid so that you can fuel your large muscles with needed oxygen. This can cause a tight feeling in your chest or a sensation of not being able to catch your breath. In addition, your muscles tense to prepare to fight or flee. The muscles in your chest tighten, and you may misinterpret that as not being able to breathe.

Sensation: Tingling or numb sensation in your face, hands, and feet

Monkey thought: *What if you become paralyzed and lose control?*

Actual cause and purpose: Blood and oxygen are being directed away from your hands, feet, and face and toward the large muscles in your legs and arms. This causes numbness and tingling. If you were actually being attacked and were injured while defending yourself, this change in circulation would help prevent you from losing too much blood.

Sensation: Nausea, nervous stomach, intestinal cramping or diarrhea, dry mouth or gag reflex

Monkey thought: *What if you throw up or don't make it to the bathroom in time?*

Actual cause and purpose: The digestion process shuts down so that more energy can go to your heart, lungs, and legs. This can cause nausea and diarrhea. If you were being attacked by a predator, you would not be eating a bag of chips. By shutting down your stomach you have more energy to run away.

Sensation: Vision changes

Monkey thought: *What if you go crazy, or things seem weird or unreal?*

Actual cause and purpose: When you are afraid, your eyes widen and your pupils dilate so that you are better able to see danger, even in darkness. This causes vision changes.

Sensation: Feeling hot and sweaty

Monkey thought: *Uh-oh—something might be wrong. You might have a panic attack and lose control!*

Actual cause and purpose: Sweat helps cool the body so that it does not overheat when you're running or fighting a threat. Also, if you're sweaty, you're more slippery to a predator, so you can get away more easily.

Sensation: Feeling cold and clammy

Monkey thought: *Uh-oh—something might be wrong. You might have a panic attack and lose control!*

Actual cause and purpose: Blood and oxygen is being directed away from your hands, feet, and face and toward the large muscles in your legs and arms. With blood moving away from your hands, if you were actually being attacked, you would be less likely to lose too much blood if injured while defending yourself.

As you can see by this list, there are good reasons for all of your panic sensations. After all, anxiety is adaptive. If we didn't feel any anxiety, our bodies wouldn't know how to respond to danger, and humankind would have been wiped out several thousand years ago. But why would your body go into fight-or-flight mode when there is no actual evidence of danger?

We don't really know. One way to think about panic attacks is that they are like a fire drill at school—a test of your fight-or-flight response to make sure it is all in working order. And like the fire alarm bell, your own body's alarms eventually go silent. Within a few minutes to a half hour at most, everything is back to normal. You feel very relieved, but of course, you also feel shaken. Unlike a fire drill, you thought it was the real deal. You thought you were really dying, going crazy, or losing control. You want very badly to leave the whole episode behind you.

Tools to Tame the Panic Monkey

In order to conquer panic, you'll need to learn how to tame the panic monkey. Fortunately, there are many tools you can reach for, and with practice, these tools will become easier and easier to use.

Spot the Thought

Since panic attacks are driven not by the situation or the sensations, but rather by your *interpretation of the sensations*, the first step to mastering panic is to identify the monkey mind interpretations, or anxious thoughts, that have been triggering your panic. Anxious thoughts are not always easy to remember, but you will uncover them by first recalling the panic sensations, which tend to be unforgettable. Make a list of all the sensations you had during your worst panic attack. (There's also a form you can use, available for download at http://www.newharbinger.com/32431.)

Next, write down what you were afraid would happen, corresponding to each sensation you listed. Good questions to ask are:

- *What popped into my mind while I was having that sensation?*

- *What am I afraid of?*

- *What is the worst that could happen?*

Monkey Miscalculations

List your monkey mind interpretations. Next to each interpretation identify the miscalculations from chapter 3 that your monkey is making. Besides the over/underestimating already mentioned, the most common monkey miscalculation behind panic attacks is catastrophizing, or leaping to the worst possible conclusion. As if watching a horror movie, the monkey mind is always imagining the worst possible outcome.

Catastrophizing

- *I am having a heart attack.*

- *I will lose control and faint.*

- *I can't breathe; I may suffocate and die.*

- *If I have a panic attack while driving I might crash the car.*

- *I feel weird; maybe I'm going crazy. What if this is schizophrenia or some other serious mental illness?*

Alternative Thoughts

Last but certainly not least, write down an alternate interpretation that is based on the actual cause and purpose of each sensation. Here is what Kim came up with:

Sensation: Tightness in chest

Monkey thought: *You can't catch your breath; you might suffocate and die.*

Monkey miscalculation: Catastrophizing

Alternative thought: *My breathing changes when I am anxious, and my muscles tense up to prepare for fight or flight. This causes my chest to feel tight.*

Sensation: Heart beating fast

Monkey thought: *Something is wrong; what if you are having a heart attack?*

Monkey miscalculation: Catastrophizing

Alternative thought: *My heart beats fast to pump blood and oxygen into my large muscles. This is part of the fight-or-flight response.*

Sensation: Light-headedness and dizziness

Monkey thought: *What if you faint?*

Monkey miscalculation: Catastrophizing

Alternative thought: *My breathing changes when I'm anxious. My body is flooded with oxygen and releases carbon dioxide, causing light-headedness. Because my blood pressure goes up, not down, during panic, I won't faint.*

By accepting the catastrophic interpretation of her uncomfortable sensations, Kim had been letting her monkey mind make decisions about how she was feeling and what she did in response. Now with Kim's alternative thoughts, she had two choices of how to respond to panic sensations—one based on fear and one based on facts.

Kim was off to a good start, and if you take the time to spot your thoughts you will be too. Once you can see the monkey mind at work, and learn to distinguish between a harmless panic feeling and a genuine threat to your health, you may find that your overall anxiety decreases a bit. (You can download an Alternative Thoughts worksheet at http://www.newharbinger.com/32431.)

More important, you have an alternative to your monkey thoughts now. There is a bigger and more rational part of your brain that knows who you really are and what your dreams and goals are. You can make decisions that are not based on fear. With an alternative way of thinking, you are ready for the next step, which will require all of your courage and presence of mind.

Kim was pretty psyched about her alternative thoughts. They helped her choose to attend a sleepover party at her best friend's house, which she would not have done before. But she was still pretty worried that she might panic, so she made sure to bring her pills with her. When she started to feel her heart racing a bit, she decided to take her medicine just to be on the safe side. She thought it was too risky to have a panic attack in front of all her friends and worried it would ruin their night. She was happy that she went to the party, but was not happy about depending on medication to get her through it.

Kim was at a crossroads. She had previously been a carefree person who enjoyed planning activities with her boyfriend, friends, and family. Now the thing she thought about the most was having another panic attack, and all her planning was based on how to avoid it. She hated being dependent on her parents to pick her up when panic struck, and she felt uncomfortable depending on her pills so much. Before, she had enjoyed doing some things alone, but now she wanted to be around people she considered safe.

Kim was also having a lot of panic-like sensations, which were increasingly uncomfortable and exhausting. She felt on edge all the time. The fun was gone from her life and her world was getting smaller. Knowing that panic sensations aren't physically dangerous wasn't enough. Kim needed to do something. But what?

Kim's problem was that her new interpretations of panic sensations, without new experience to support them, remained just thoughts. She was never going to actually *believe* she could master a panic attack unless she actually mastered one. She was going to have to stop her avoidance cycle and face the very feelings she was most afraid of.

Tools to Rule the Panic Monkey

All the tools in the world won't change the fact that facing panic is scary. Our first tool addresses the big question, *Are the things I am missing out on by avoiding panic worth fighting for?*

Life Compass

Kim had lost her sense of direction in life. Following her monkey and avoiding her panic was sending her south every time. To help her find her true north again, Kim made a list of the things she used to have that she'd lost due to panic.

Not needing meds

Enjoying being alone

Not needing parents to pick me up

Going places I used to enjoy

When she looked at all the things she was missing, Kim felt they were worth fighting for, even if she was scared.

Are you willing to fight for what you are missing out on? It will mean facing your biggest fear—your own physical sensations. And you won't just wait around for them to happen, maybe hoping they won't. You will face them intentionally. Yes, in order to master panic, you must bring these sensations on *intentionally*. You will have to feel the sensations you associate with panic *on purpose*.

Can you hear your little monkey beginning to howl? It is probably telling you this is the worst idea since the atomic bomb, that it's just plain dumb. You can acknowledge your monkey by thanking it for trying to keep you safe, and at the same time recognize that the cost of doing things the monkey mind way is just too high—it is time to take back control of your life. Remember, you will not be diving into a pool of panic, but rather wading in with small, manageable steps.

You can download a Life Compass worksheet at http://www.newharbinger.com/32431.

The Challenge Ladder

As you learned in chapter 4, the best way to think about facing your fears is with a ladder that reaches toward the life you want to live. Kim's goals all pointed toward one big idea: to gain back her independence from medication and enjoy doing the things she had always liked to do. To determine what challenge rungs would help her meet these goals, the question she needs to ask is, *What have I been avoiding?*

What you are actually avoiding with panic attacks are your own sensations. Kim identified each of her panic sensations and ranked them in order of scariness, with 10 being the most scary and 1 being the least. Here's what she got:

- Tightness in chest: 10

- Heart beating fast: 8

- Light-headed and dizzy: 7

- Hot and sweaty: 5

In order for Kim to face these sensations in a purposeful way, and in a time and place of her choosing, she would have to bring them on intentionally. Here are some specific exercises and the panic sensations they can cause:

Exercise: Hyperventilate. Breathe in and out quickly for anywhere from fifteen seconds to one minute, taking short breaks.

Effect: Light-headedness; increased heart rate; heart palpitations; tightness in chest; feeling hot and sweaty; feeling cold and clammy; tingly sensation in your face, hands, and feet; and difficulty breathing.

Exercise: Do any brisk exercise, such as jumping jacks or going up and down stairs, for two to five minutes.

Effect: Increased heart rate, tightness in chest, feeling hot and sweaty, and difficulty breathing.

Exercise: Put your head between your knees and shake it back and forth for thirty seconds, then bring your head up quickly. Or spin around, either sitting in a spinning chair or standing up, for thirty seconds to one minute.

Effect: Dizziness, light-headedness, vision changes.

Exercise: Stare at your mouth in the mirror while repeating a nursery rhyme over and over again for one to five minutes. Or stare at the same spot on the wall without moving your eyes away for one to five minutes.

Effect: Vision changes or a feeling of detachment or unreality.

For the lowest rung on her ladder Kim chose the sensation that made her the least anxious: "hot and sweaty."

Kim knew that facing her panic would be less overwhelming at home, with her parents nearby, so she started off there. Here's what her challenge ladder looked like when she was done:

Goals:
Gain back my independence and confidence. Enjoy doing the things I've always liked to do. Not be dependent on medication.

Jumping jacks for 2 min. with a 1 min. break 10 times at home with parents away

Jumping jacks for 2 min. with a 2 min. break 10 times at home with parents away

Jumping jacks for 2 min. with a 2 min. break 10 times at home with parents home

Jumping jacks for 2 min. with a 2 min. break 5 times at home with parents away

Jumping jacks for 2 min. with a 2 min. break 5 times at home with parents at home

Jumping jacks for 1 min. with a 1 min. break 5 times at home with parents away

Jumping jacks for 1 min. with a 1 min. break 5 times at home with parents home

This is a great first ladder. Once Kim was able to reach the top, she could make a similar ladder for the next sensations that she had been avoiding: dizziness and light-headedness. To face these sensations she could put her head between her knees, shake it, and then bring it up quickly. Next, she could move on to hyperventilating.

Of course, this would be easier in the planning than in the doing. But Kim was determined, and she had a secret weapon to try—welcoming the sensations and the anxiety.

You can download a Challenge Ladder for Panic worksheet at http://www.newharbinger.com/32431.

Acceptance

Imagine for a minute that you are thrown into the middle of a vast sea. You flail your arms and kick your legs to keep from sinking, and at first it seems to work, but as you begin to tire the effect is just the opposite. To stay afloat you must spread your arms and legs as far apart as you can and fill your lungs. By accepting and welcoming the water, rather than resisting it, you can stay afloat indefinitely.

As you meet your first challenge you will start to feel sensations that are uncomfortable or that you associate with panic. Your first instinct will be to tighten up, clench your stomach, tense your muscles, and get up and move around. Remember that you are not to fight these sensations. Fighting these sensations is what got you into trouble in the first place. What you resist, persists.

By resisting uncomfortable sensations you are agreeing with your monkey that these sensations are dangerous. To master your panic, do the opposite of your instincts and accept your uncomfortable sensations.

Welcoming Breath

As you have learned, when we get anxious, our breathing becomes shallow and fast. This type of breathing creates all sorts of physiological changes and has the effect of intensifying physical sensations, so that you end up resisting them even more, and breathing more quickly and shallowly. Breathing this way tells your body that you agree with your monkey: *Something is wrong!*

To welcome anxious sensations rather than resisting them, breathe in the opposite way:

1. Breathe in deeply, filling your lungs so that your belly softens and expands.

2. Breathe out completely so that your belly contracts.

3. Repeat slowly and deliberately.

By consciously choosing to breathe slowly and steadily you are telling your body, *I can handle this.* Breathing this way will help you ride out the intense and uncomfortable waves of sensation. And it has the additional benefit of training your monkey, which gets no banana when you welcome the anxiety it warned you about.

Remember that you are not trying to relax. Relaxation techniques, like imagining yourself on a peaceful beach, are based on the idea that your uncomfortable sensations are bad and must be stopped. If you've ever tried that technique, you know it doesn't work.

As you welcome panic sensations with your breath, whether you find yourself feeling less anxious or find yourself feeling more anxious doesn't matter. The point is that you are accepting the feelings. You are showing yourself that feeling bad isn't dangerous. It is simply part of life—a part you are willing to experience when it comes up. This is how you rule the monkey and master panic.

Kim worked hard at climbing her ladder. Within twelve weeks she was much less afraid of having a panic attack. When she would get waves of panic sensations she was able to recognize them as harmless. This did not mean that she liked them, but they did not scare her like they had before. Consequently, she was having way fewer panic attacks. In fact, they didn't feel much like panic attacks anymore. They were milder, and fewer and farther between.

Kim's hard work changed her relationship with anxiety and with her monkey. When she did get a feeling of anxiety she immediately went to her welcoming breath. By learning to accept panic, she mastered it and her world opened up.

With this knowledge and these tools, you can go anywhere you want to go. Where do *you* want to go? What are you waiting for?

Agoraphobia

The word *agoraphobia* sounds kind of scary and it is often misunderstood. Most people think of agoraphobia as a fear of leaving your house. This specific fear can be part of it, but it is not the definition of agoraphobia.

Agoraphobia is the fear of having some kind of an attack in a place or situation where escape would be difficult or embarrassing, or when help might not be immediately available. It could be a panic attack, loss of bowel or bladder control, dizziness, fainting, throwing up, an asthma attack, a headache, or some other extreme pain. In other words, agoraphobia is the fear of having an attack and being trapped.

Common situations that trigger the fear of being trapped are being on a plane, in a car, on a bridge, or in a movie theater or classroom far away from an exit. It is not a fear of the plane crashing or of the height of the bridge—those would be specific phobias. Rather, an agoraphobic teen would be afraid of having an attack and being trapped on a plane or bridge.

Some people with agoraphobia have a fear of taking medicine—again, not because they are afraid of choking, which is a specific phobia, but because they feel that once the medicine is in their body they will be trapped and have to wait for any possible side effects from it to go away. It is also common for people with agoraphobia to worry if they are a certain distance from their home, a hospital, or a bathroom. They may also worry about being alone. About one out of three people who have a problem with panic attacks will develop agoraphobia.

To free yourself from agoraphobia you would use the same steps as for panic attacks. You can learn more about agoraphobia from other resources listed in the appendix at the end of this book.

Chapter 8

Specific Phobias

Insects, Vomit, and Needles—Yikes!

Back in fourth grade, when Anton was ten, one of his classmates threw up on the floor of the bus on a field trip. Ever since then Anton was petrified of getting the stomach flu. He avoided riding on the school bus except when going to and from school, which was only a short distance. He refused to ride the bus for field trips, so either his parents drove him or he wouldn't go at all. If someone at school complained of feeling sick, Anton would begin to panic and would avoid that person as much as possible. He constantly checked his own body for signs of nausea, and whenever he felt hungry or too full he worried the discomfort might be a sign he was getting sick. Anton also worried about eating food that might make him sick, so he always checked expiration dates and wanted to know how long food had been sitting out before he ate it. He carried antacids with him to settle his stomach. Worst of all, Anton often had trouble going to sleep at night because he was worried he might wake up in the middle of the night vomiting.

A nton has a specific phobia, which means that he has an extreme fear of a specific thing or situation. Justin, whom you met in chapter 2, had a specific phobia of dogs. Anton's phobia is centered around vomit.

Phobias are very common. In fact, most people have some type of phobia. Being frightened by things is part of being human. But when your phobia stops you from doing what you want to do or going where you want to go, it's a real problem.

This is what was happening for Anton. He couldn't eat at certain restaurants that were popular with his friends for fear he might get sick from the food. He couldn't go on long car trips because he was worried he might get carsick. He wouldn't go near any of his friends if they or anyone in their family had been sick recently. His phobia was keeping him from living life the way he wanted to live it.

Specific phobias can be about almost anything, but here are some of the most common types:

- Animals: dogs, cats, mice, rats, birds, snakes, insects

- Things that occur in the natural environment: heights, water, thunderstorms, or lightning

- Situations and places: traveling in a car, plane, bus, train, or boat; closed-in spaces such as closets and tunnels

- Medical issues: injuries, blood, needles, dentists, doctors, hospitals

- Illness and bodily functions: vomiting, stomach flu, food poisoning, choking on pills or food, having a dry or closed throat, not being able to breathe

Like all anxiety, specific phobias are rooted in our fundamental need to survive. There are plenty of animals—even insects—that can kill you. People *do* drown, die from falling, and get struck by lightning. Accidents *do* happen to people traveling in cars and planes. If you were trapped in a tight space, you *could* die. Blood, injuries, needles, hospitals, vomiting, and choking are all associated with death. And staying alive, as we know, is the brain's number one job.

But although phobias originate from potential threats, they are unrealistic and exaggerated. For the anxious teen, the part of the brain that decides what is dangerous—what we call the monkey mind—is hyperactive and overly threat-sensitive. It makes a classic miscalculation. It 1) overestimates the threat and 2) underestimates your ability to deal with it. This assessment of the danger amounts to little more than a wild guess.

So why is your monkey mind making wild guesses about your specific phobia? You can't really know. The genetics you were born with and the behavior your parents or caretaker modeled for you may have had an influence. There also may have been a bad experience that triggered your phobia.

Justin, from chapter 2, developed a fear of dogs after being attacked by one. If you saw or read about a terrible plane crash or someone getting struck by lightning, you may have developed a fear of the same thing happening to you. Or you may have been trained to be extra cautious about something. From an early age, even before he developed his fear of vomiting, Anton's mother told him to breathe through his nose whenever he was around people who were sick.

Regardless of how your phobia originated, the problem is the same. When you are confronted with your phobia your monkey mind sets off your anxiety alarm and you find yourself in fight-or-flight mode. You feel the threat is real, and you do whatever it takes to avoid it. Then, when nothing bad happens, your monkey takes credit for keeping you safe, reinforcing the wild guess it made about the danger in the first place, which starts the whole process again. This is the *cycle of avoidance* that keeps all anxiety going.

If Anton stays away from his best friend who is sick with the flu, and then does not himself get sick, his monkey mind decides, *Because you avoided your friend, you didn't get sick and throw up!*

Here are some typical examples of monkey logic about different phobias:

Monkey thought: *What if a spider jumps down on you at night and bites you in your sleep?*

Avoidant behavior: Look around the bed and corners of the room to make sure there are no spiders.

Monkey logic: *Because you made sure there were no spiders you did not get bitten.*

Monkey thought: *If you get a shot it will hurt really, really bad and you won't be able to stand it!*

Avoidant behavior: Don't go to the doctor or dentist.

Monkey logic: *Because you didn't get a shot, you didn't have to endure horrible pain.*

Monkey thought: *What if you get struck by lightning?*

Avoidant behavior: Don't go outside if it's raining or cloudy.

Monkey logic: *Because you didn't go out, you did not get struck by lightning.*

Monkey thought: *What if a piece of popcorn gets stuck in your throat and you can't breathe?*

Avoidant behavior: Avoid eating popcorn, or eat popcorn but always have a drink ready in case it gets stuck in your throat.

Monkey logic: *Because you didn't eat popcorn or had water nearby, you didn't choke and die.*

Monkey thought: *If you go on an elevator it might get stuck and you'll never get out.*

Avoidant behavior: Take the stairs instead.

Monkey logic: *Because you took the stairs, you didn't get trapped in the elevator.*

Tools to Tame the Phobia Monkey

Once your monkey mind decides something is dangerous—spiders or heights or your own closet, it doesn't matter—it sounds the alarm, putting you in fight-or-flight mode. When your body is flooded with fear, even the wild guesses of your monkey mind can actually feel true. So how do you know if the thing you're afraid of is actually dangerous or not?

Monkey Miscalculations

You can always tell a monkey thought by its miscalculations. Monkeys just aren't very good at assessing risk. In addition to the classic over/underestimating miscalculation, with specific phobias the following three miscalculations are usually found:

1. **Catastrophizing:** The monkey mind imagines the worst that could happen.

   - *What if you get bitten by a rattlesnake while hiking?*

   - *It is storming; what if you get struck by lightning?*

   - *What if the bridge collapses while you are driving across it?*

   - *What if a pill gets stuck in your throat and you choke to death?*

2. **Discounting the positive:** Your monkey forgets all the times you have been in your feared situation and nothing bad happened. How many times have you walked past bees and not been stung, or felt nauseous and not thrown up, or been in an elevator that did not get stuck? Too many to count. But your monkey mind will not take good outcomes into consideration. Its job is to detect threat, no matter how unlikely—which takes us to the last monkey miscalculation.

3. **Intolerance of uncertainty:** If there is even a .01 percent chance that something terrible could happen, your monkey will not rest. A great example is the fear of flying. Airplanes are by far the safest way to travel, with the odds of you dying in a plane crash at one in 11 million. Yet fear of flying is quite common.

Spot the Thought

Monkey miscalculations, like all thoughts, happen pretty quickly. If you have any difficulty figuring out exactly what the thought is that triggers your phobia, try this exercise. Ask yourself these two questions: *What am I afraid of?* and *What's the worst that could happen if this were true?*

Here's how Anton answered:

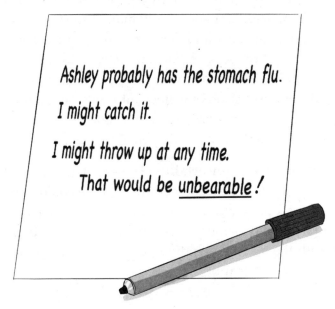

Ashley probably has the stomach flu.

I might catch it.

I might throw up at any time.

That would be unbearable !

Once Anton had his thoughts spelled out in front of him, he realized he was making all of these specific phobia monkey miscalculations. Assuming that Ashley had the flu and that he would get it too was overestimating the threat. By assuming that throwing up would be unbearable for him, he was catastrophizing and underestimating his ability to cope. By forgetting all the times that others felt sick and he did not throw up, he was discounting the positive. And when Ashley said she felt sick, he jumped to conclusions instead of tolerating the uncertainty of whether or not he would catch it and throw up.

Recognizing these miscalculations made Anton feel a little bit better. Though he wasn't certain it would help him feel any different the next time a similar situation came up, it did allow him to distance himself from his monkey mind. He would have to gauge the actual risk that was presented by Ashley's feeling sick.

You can download a Spot the Thought worksheet for phobias at http://www.newharbinger.com/32431.

Collect the Data

As any scientist will tell you, to make accurate predictions about the future you must look at past results. Scientists collect and analyze lots of data before they come up with a theory. Monkeys are not scientists; they can only make what are, at best, wild guesses and then push the alarm button. You, however, are capable of collecting and evaluating data. You can determine how likely you are to be hurt by the thing you are afraid of, rather than relying on the wild guesses of a monkey.

For the next week Anton kept a list of the times he felt nauseous—what he was thinking at the time and what actually happened. At the end of the week he reviewed his data.

He had an incidence of feeling nauseous at least once a day—after eating cafeteria pizza, after missing a meal, while smelling something cooking, or while just lying in bed. He noticed that in each incidence his monkey mind told him some variation of the same prediction: *You might be sick. You're going to throw up!*

But Anton didn't throw up that week. He realized that his monkey had predicted he would throw up at least once a day for years, ever since that field trip when he was ten. In fact, in his entire life Anton could remember only two times he had actually thrown up. Based on past performance, his monkey's chance of making a correct prediction was about one in a thousand!

Have you looked at the data for your specific phobia? For example, if you have a phobia of bees, can you calculate how many times you have come into contact with a bee and how many times you were actually stung? No matter what your specific phobia, when you collect and compare the data you'll see that your monkey's predictions almost never match the results.

You can download a Collect the Data on Your Phobia worksheet at http://www.newharbinger.com/32431.

Educate Yourself

Another great way to tame your monkey is to educate yourself about whatever it is you're afraid of. If you are afraid of flying, for example, google "airplane safety." If you are worried about poisonous snakes, find out what types of snakes actually can be found in your area and what the death rate is for bites.

The more you spot your thoughts, identify monkey miscalculations, collect data, and educate yourself, the less reliable your monkey mind will seem and the less compelling its alarms for your safety. Most likely, you will then feel less anxious. You may even stop avoiding the thing you've been afraid of.

If your anxiety is still so intense that you are avoiding, read on for tools that will help you further tame the little critter.

Tools to Rule the Phobia Monkey

All the work you do identifying your monkey thoughts won't help if you continue to play by your monkey's rules. Every time you respond to a monkey alarm by avoiding the supposed threat, you are in effect giving it a banana. To rule your monkey you must ignore its false alarms and actually move toward what you are afraid of. This will not be easy. In fact, it may be the hardest thing you've ever done.

Life Compass

Perhaps this is a good time to ask yourself whether overcoming your phobia is important enough for you to tolerate the anxiety that will come up in the process. What is your avoidance costing you? What are you missing out on? Are these things worth fighting for?

Trish was afraid of spiders, and she came up with the following list of things her fear cost her:

I can't go camping with my friends.

I waste time checking for spiders before getting into bed or the shower.

I waste time worrying about whether there is a spider nearby.

Trish decided it was worth it to begin to face her fear of spiders. Not being able to go camping with friends was the deal-breaker.

Dan was afraid of elevators. His list looked like this:

I'm embarrassed with friends because I am not able to use elevators.

I can't go to upper floors if there are too many stairs to climb.

He decided it was not really worth it to face his fear. He was able to avoid elevators pretty easily, and although his fear was embarrassing, his friends still liked him.

Here's Anton's list:

Eating certain foods or at restaurants

Being around people who might be sick

Going places that require a long car ride

Hours and hours wasted on worrying

For Anton, the decision was clear. His phobia affected him every day, everywhere he went. It would be worth facing his anxiety to be able to hang out with his friends, eat at restaurants, and go on long car trips. Anton was ready to start ruling his monkey.

To help you decide whether it's worth it to face your phobia, you can download a Life Compass worksheet at http://www.newharbinger.com/32431.

The Challenge Ladder

If you have a fear of heights you won't go straight to the Grand Canyon and stand on the edge. If you're afraid of bees you won't start out by visiting a bee farm. Ruling your monkey is best accomplished by taking small, manageable steps toward what you are afraid of—like climbing a ladder.

Take trips and go to
restaurants with my friends

Watch YouTube videos
of people throwing up

Listen to sounds of
people throwing up

Look at photos of
people throwing up

Look at cartoon pictures
of people throwing up

Say or look at words like
barf, throw up, and puke

Each step on your ladder will be a challenge that you can meet without being overwhelmed. As you meet each challenge you will learn to ignore the howls of your monkey and gain confidence in your own assessment of the danger.

Anton's fear of vomiting was so overwhelming that even hearing or saying the word made him anxious. That sounded like a good challenge for the first rung of his ladder.

Here are some ideas for challenge ladders for other types of phobias:

Fear of Animals

- Looking at pictures, cartoons, or color photos of an animal you're afraid of

- Listening to recorded sounds of the animal—such as a dog growling or barking, a snake hissing, or birds chirping

- Watching videos of the animal

- Going to a pet store

- Looking at the animal when it's contained in some way (such as a dog on a leash or a snake or rodent in a glass container at a pet store)

- Touching the animal

Fear of Heights

- Standing on a chair

- Climbing a ladder

- Climbing a tree

- Going up the floors of a building, one at a time

- Looking down from a high building through a window, then from an open window, then from a balcony
- Going on a Ferris wheel

Fear of Storms

- Looking at pictures of storms and lightning
- Listening to sounds of rain, thunder, and lightning
- Looking at videos of rain, thunder, and lightning
- Standing by an open window while it is raining or storming outside
- Going outside when it's cloudy, then when it's raining, then during a thunderstorm

Claustrophobia, or Fear of Being Trapped

- Going into a closet with the door open
- Going into a closet with the door closed
- Wrapping a blanket tightly around yourself
- Putting a heavy blanket over your head
- Standing in an elevator with the doors closed for a long period of time
- Sitting in the back seat of a car with only two doors
- Going into an attic or crawl space

Fear of Doctors, Blood, or Needles

- Reading or listening to words like "blood," "injury," "shot," "needle," "syringe," "dentist," "drilling," "doctor," and "surgery"

- Looking at cartoon pictures then actual color photos of blood or needles

- Going to dentists' or doctors' waiting rooms, or visiting a hospital

- Making fake blood, putting it on your body or someone else's body, and looking at it

- Going to a blood drive and watching blood getting drawn

- Looking at and handling syringes or dentist's tools

- Reading about medical procedures, or watching TV shows or movies about them

- Watching someone get blood drawn, getting your blood drawn, or getting a shot

- Sitting in a dentist chair, getting your teeth cleaned, or getting a cavity filled

You can download a Challenge Ladder worksheet at http://www.newharbinger.com/32431.

Applied Tension

If you have ever fainted or felt light-headed or dizzy at the sight of needles or blood, it is very likely that you experienced a sudden drop in blood pressure. It would be a good idea to see a doctor to make sure there is nothing else going on. You can make yourself less susceptible to passing out at the sight of needles or blood by using *applied tension*, a simple technique that raises your blood pressure and can prevent fainting. Do it twice a day for one week before starting your challenge ladder.

Applied Tension Instructions

Sit in a chair and tense your arms, legs, and stomach. You can tense your arms by making fists and holding your arms bent at your sides. And you can tense your legs by sticking them straight out in front of you. For your stomach, imagine that someone just threw a ball at you and hold your muscles tight. Do these all at once and hold for ten to fifteen seconds, then relax for thirty seconds. Repeat this five times. You may feel pressure in your head when you do this. That is fine—it lets you know the exercise is working.

Once you have done this for one week, you can start your challenge ladder, while at the same time practicing applied tension. If you get to the point where you no longer feel faint while doing your challenges, you may discontinue doing applied tension.

Like Anton, you've been ruled by monkey thoughts for a long time, perhaps years. Learning how to tolerate the anxiety that comes when you stop avoiding will take practice, so be patient with yourself.

Acceptance

As you approach each challenge, you will likely feel the urge to "white-knuckle" it—holding your breath, gritting your teeth, and hanging on to the handrail, hoping to get through it as fast as possible. When you white-knuckle your way through a challenge, your monkey is still in charge. You are still avoiding what might happen and resisting getting too anxious.

Your goal during each challenge is to completely accept whatever feelings come up. This is the exact opposite of everything you have been doing up until now. You've always

avoided your phobia; your challenge now is to face your phobia instead. This means getting anxious on purpose—and when you do get anxious, to allow the anxiety to be there without doing anything to get rid of it. This is what we mean by acceptance— unconditional surrender.

Your challenges will work much better if you go into them saying, *I am ready to face this fear and I want to get as anxious as possible!* This is very confusing for your monkey. You've been rewarding it for saving you from anxiety. Every time it predicts disaster and sounds the alarm, you've been giving it a banana. When you ignore the alarm and welcome anxiety you are playing by *your* rules, not your monkey's!

Welcoming Breath

To control and avoid anxiety, people tense up by either holding their breath or breathing too quickly. Or they use their breath to try to relax. By tensing up or trying to relax, you are not letting your anxiety run its course. You are actually agreeing with your monkey that anxiety is a danger signal that you need to do something about. When you are meeting a challenge by tensing up or trying to relax you are not really meeting your challenge.

To welcome anxiety you must learn to breathe *into* it—the very opposite of what you've been doing. To see what I mean, imagine the thing you are afraid of in detail, enough to get your anxiety to at least a 5 on a 1-to-10 scale. Don't read any further until you are there.

Feeling uncomfortable? Good! Now do the following:

1. Breathe in deeply, filling your lungs so that your belly expands.

2. Breathe out completely.

3. Repeat slowly and deliberately.

By breathing into your anxiety, you are telling your monkey that anxiety is nothing to be afraid of. You are opening up your body to give the anxiety room to play itself out. This is something you've never done before, so it probably sounds scary. But not allowing yourself to actually feel anxiety is why your anxiety is still haunting you. What you resist, persists.

What you will find when you keep welcoming and keep breathing is that your anxious feelings will begin to change on their own. At first, your fear may feel stronger, as if it will overwhelm and destroy you. That's what your monkey mind will be telling you, anyway! But feeling fear cannot hurt you. Your body is designed to feel things, and there is no emotion that can physically hurt you.

Anton began his challenges by simply saying the words "vomit," "puke," "throw up," and so on. He kept track of how anxious that made him feel, and after only three sessions saying those words repeatedly only got him to 1 on a 1-to-10 anxiety scale. But when he began looking at cartoons of people throwing up, his anxiety went up to a 7. He looked at the cartoons every day, and by the end of the week he still felt somewhat disgusted by the pictures. But his anxiety was down to a 2.

Photographic images of people throwing up pushed Anton's anxiety up to a 9. Some of the pictures were really bad, so he had his dad help him pick out pictures that were less disgusting to start with. After a few days he was able to look at the worst of them without his anxiety going beyond a 3.

When the challenges made Anton feel sick to his stomach he noticed that his anxiety increased. His monkey mind was chattering away, telling him he was about to throw up. Of course, Anton knew the odds of that happening were slim. He'd only thrown up twice in his entire life! The longer he did the challenge and did not throw up, the more his anxiety went down.

Anton decided he was ready to move on to listening to sounds of people throwing up. He got his dad to pick out YouTube videos of people throwing up. He covered the screen of his computer so that he did not see the images, and set the videos to replay over and over. When his anxiety went down to a 2 he began watching the images along with the sound. It did not take him as long to get used to this as he had thought it would. His disgust never really went away, but he was much less anxious.

All of this ladder practice was helping Anton throughout the day. Whenever a friend showed any sign of being sick, he still got anxious, but the urge to run was much less strong than before, and he found that he could breathe his way through it. The challenges were giving him confidence and conviction that feeling nauseous was not the same as throwing up.

One day some friends invited him to a concert that was a two-hour drive away. Even though it meant being in a car all that time and eating at strange places, to Anton's own surprise he said yes. It just didn't feel that scary anymore. Life is looking good for Anton!

Many people go their whole lives carefully avoiding something that, on its own, holds no actual threat. They may rationalize it by saying that it really doesn't inconvenience them that much, but in their hearts they know they long for the freedom of choosing their own paths without being detoured by fear.

You don't have to resign yourself this way. You have the tools to rule your monkey. Remember that you are not alone and not to blame. Have compassion for yourself and take courage. You can live the life you want to live!

Chapter 9

Generalized Anxiety

Worrywarts

Tess was known as a "worrywart" from the time she was little. She worried about almost anything, from a mosquito bite causing West Nile disease to a B on a test ruining her chances of getting into college. She felt stressed out nearly all the time, and she frequently had headaches and stomachaches. Things were really bad at night, when there was nothing to distract her from worrying. Her thoughts were like a mouse on a wheel, going around and around. She often had trouble falling asleep, and when she finally did she would feel restless throughout the night, waking up tired and irritable.

Tess has generalized anxiety. Instead of having fears about something specific—like spiders, or being judged, or having a panic attack—she has fears that are more general. Teens with general anxiety worry about school, work, family, health, and things going on in the world.

These kinds of worries are about things that really could happen, which can make things confusing. After all, if you have a bad feeling about something happening, shouldn't you pay attention to it?

Anxiety *can* be a signal to pay attention to a problem so you can solve it and prevent something bad from happening. But like the hunter who thought every track on the ground was a saber-toothed tiger track, if you suffer from generalized anxiety you will get so many danger signals that you spend countless hours trying to solve problems that you've already solved or that are beyond your control. Chronic worry is not useful and is something nobody wants. Teens with this type of anxiety say the same thing: "Please help me stop worrying!"

When you have generalized anxiety, your monkey mind is looking out at the world through binoculars. Small things get blown out of proportion and your monkey jumps to the worst-case scenario. The resulting worry you experience is exhausting and actually interferes with your ability to concentrate. This is worry that does not help keep you safe.

Like all anxiety, generalized anxiety is maintained by avoidance. You may make endless lists to avoid forgetting anything. You may ask for reassurance from friends, parents, or doctors that there is nothing wrong with you. You may put off decisions in order to avoid making the wrong one. Perhaps you avoid the possibility of getting a bad grade by over-studying.

Sometimes the only thing you are doing is worrying. How is that avoidance? People with generalized anxiety believe that worrying will help them be more prepared if things turn out badly, or that if they worry long enough they will eventually come up with a solution that will keep them safe. It feels better to worry than to feel the discomfort of not knowing what will happen. Worry is an attempt to eliminate risk and thus reduce anxiety.

Let's take Tess's anxious thought: *What if that mosquito that just bit me is carrying West Nile virus?* This is a scary thought. But it is something Tess can't do anything about, and when she begins to worry about that possibility she is giving the thought more attention than it deserves. She is feeding her monkey a banana, telling it that the thought is important. As long as she keeps worrying about the worst possible outcome of her mosquito bite, and looking for reassurance that it will not happen, Tess is fueling her cycle of avoidance.

To make matters worse, when the outcome you are afraid of does not happen (because most of the things people with generalized anxiety worry about are highly unlikely), your monkey takes full credit. Monkey logic says, *Because you worried about West Nile disease, you didn't get West Nile disease.*

Let's take a look at the role of the monkey mind in other examples of generalized worry.

Monkey thought: *What if your headaches are caused by a brain tumor?*

Avoidant behavior: Worry. Ask to see a doctor. Look up other symptoms of brain tumors on the Internet.

Monkey logic: *Because you are keeping an eye on things, you are less likely to die from a brain tumor.*

Monkey thought: *What if your parents get divorced? Your life will be ruined!*

Avoidant behavior: Worry. Ask parents if everything is okay.

Monkey logic: *Because you are worrying and checking in with your parents, you will be prepared if anything bad happens.*

Monkey thought: *What if you forget something important? That will ruin everything!*

Avoidant behavior: Worry. Mentally review things that you need to remember. Make lots of lists.

Monkey logic: *Because you made lists and did not forget anything, nothing terrible happened. You saved the day!*

Monkey thought: *You might die in a car accident!*

Avoidant behavior: Worry. Tell whoever is driving the car to slow down. Look to see if other drivers on the road might be drunk.

Monkey logic: *Because you worried and watched out for danger, you did not get in a car accident. You avoided catastrophe!*

When you worry over things you've already taken steps to prepare for, or things that are beyond your control, you reward monkey logic. You are giving your monkey a banana. And there's no better way to guarantee your monkey will come up with another anxious thought about another scary outcome! It's the cycle of avoidance that keeps your worry going strong.

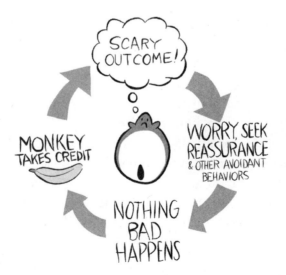

Oh, and by the way, if the thing you are worrying about *should* actually happen, the monkey mind will still get a banana. Regardless of whether the worrying was helpful, monkey logic says, *See, I told you! Good thing you prepared yourself by worrying!*

Yes, it is true that we need to prepare ourselves for threats and prevent bad things from happening. Anxiety can be a great heads-up that you need to do something about a problematic situation. But once you have done that, repeating the process over and over—otherwise known as worrying—is useless. All it does is feed the monkey mind and create more anxiety.

Tools to Tame the Generalized Anxiety Monkey

The challenge with worry is to tell the difference between anxious thoughts that are an important signal of a problem needing to be solved, and anxious thoughts that are monkey chatter. Thinking that a mosquito bite will result in West Nile disease is monkey chatter. Even if it were true, there is nothing that you could do about it in the moment.

Here is a list of situations. Some are examples of a call to action—to either prevent or cope with a bad situation. Others are examples of monkey chatter—meaning something could go wrong but either 1) there is no way to solve the problem or 2) you have already solved it but are still worrying about it. Read each situation and determine whether it is a solvable problem or monkey chatter. (The answers will be provided at the end.)

a. You are worried that because you have not studied you may not do well on your history exam tomorrow.

b. You worry that your parents might get a divorce.

c. You have studied until midnight but you still are worried that you won't do well on your test tomorrow.

d. You worry that you might get the stomach flu and your weekend plans will be ruined.

e. You worry that you did not do well in the job interview and you may not get the job you really wanted.

f. You have sent in your college applications but you are worried that you won't get into the colleges you want to.

g. You remembered that you forgot your friend's birthday and may have hurt her feelings.

h. It is late at night and you're worrying about the possibility that your boyfriend or girlfriend will break up with you.

i. Your sister just got her driver's license and you worry she might get in a car accident.

j. Your friend is texting while driving and you worry that he might get in a car accident.

Answers:

a. Solvable problem. If you have not studied there is something you could do about that before your test the next day.

b. Chatter. Whether or not this is true there is nothing you can do about it.

c. Chatter. You have already studied, and while it may be true that you don't know everything, worrying about that is not going to help.

d. Chatter. How is worrying about this going to help? You either will or won't get sick. There is nothing you can do about it.

e. Chatter. You already had the interview. There is nothing you can do at this point. It is up to them to decide if they will hire you or not.

f. Chatter. You already sent off your applications. There is nothing you can do at this point.

g. Solvable problem. You could always call your friend to wish her a late happy birthday. If you do this but still worry about it, then it becomes chatter, because you did what you could and you can't control how your friend feels.

h. Chatter. It is late at night—what can you do about this now? If there is something going on in the relationship that needs attention you can talk with that person the next day.

i. Chatter. While it is true that newly licensed drivers are more at risk, there is nothing you can do about this. Remember, everyone starts out as a newly licensed driver!

j. Solvable problem. It is dangerous to text and drive, and you have every right to ask your friend to stop.

Your own worrisome situations may not be on this list, and they may feel unique to you. Fortunately there are powerful tools you can use to recognize the chatter and tame the monkey.

Spot the Thought

There are three basic questions to ask yourself:

1. *What am I afraid of?*

2. *What is the worst that could happen if this were true?*

3. *What would this mean about me, my life, or my future?*

Here are Tess's answers:

1. I might not get a good grade on this test.

2. It could affect my GPA and I might not get into a good college.

3. I could wind up without a career, even homeless!

Before you go any further, take a moment to spot a thought of your own. You can download a "Spot the Thought" worksheet for generalized anxiety at http://www .newharbinger.com/32431.

Monkey Miscalculations

When you look at things people worry about, there is usually plenty of evidence of that classic monkey miscalculation: over/underestimating. You can see it in the worries shown in the monkey logic examples earlier in this chapter.

Being killed in a car accident is very unlikely, and not getting into college just because you did poorly on a test is not very likely either. To worry about these outcomes is to overestimate the risk of them happening.

What about the chances of your parents getting a divorce, or that you forget an assignment? These are not only overestimations of danger but underestimations of your ability to handle it if those things did happen. Whether your monkey is overestimating risk or underestimating your ability to cope—or both—the result is the same. Your monkey tells you to *Worry! Worry a lot! It's your only chance to be prepared or to prevent something bad from happening!*

Here are two other monkey miscalculations commonly found with generalized worry.

Catastrophizing

There are lots of possible outcomes to any situation, but the monkey mind always assumes the worst. Naturally, this makes you feel on edge much of the time, and you'll work overtime to prepare for and prevent anything bad from happening.

Do any of these catastrophic monkey thoughts sound familiar?

- *Your stomach hurts. It might be salmonella poisoning!*

- *If you forget something for your trip, it will be ruined!*

- *Your mom has been tired lately. What if she has cancer?*

- *If you ever got detention it would be terrible!*

Intolerance of Uncertainty

No matter how the odds favor a positive result, if there is even the thinnest sliver of a chance that something could go wrong, the monkey mind cannot rest. Instead of assuming that you are safe unless there are clear signs of danger, the monkey mind will assume danger unless there is 100 percent safety. Since it is impossible to be 100 percent safe, you will worry endlessly, striving for the impossible.

Alternative Thoughts

Before you spend another minute worrying about something, why not take a critical look at the thought that is triggering that worry? If you look at the evidence *for* the thought being true, as well as the evidence *against* it being true, you'll have a better idea whether what you are dealing with is a genuine threat or just another monkey thought.

Here's Tess's "Evidence For and Against" exercise about the threat that getting a B on a test will mean she won't get into a good college and may end up homeless. As you can see, it led her to a more balanced alternative thought about getting a B that gave her a lot less cause to worry.

Evidence For: It is true I got a B on the test. Grades on tests affect final grades in the class, and final grades affect grade point averages. Colleges look at grade point averages.

Evidence Against: This test was only 20 percent of my overall grade in the class. I have an A average in the class so far, so this B won't affect my final grade unless I get a B or lower on the next test. Even if my final grade is a B, I will still have a good GPA and could get into many good colleges.

Alternative Thought: *While it is true that test grades can affect final grades, I would have to do poorly from now on to get a bad grade in the class. Even if I did get a bad grade, I could still get into good colleges.*

When you use this tool, make sure that you stick to the facts. When Tess was gathering evidence for and against, she could have said, *I might get bad grades from now on.* This is not a fact, only something that could happen in the future. The facts were: she had an A average so far, and this test accounted for 20 percent of her final grade. Sticking with facts sometimes means you will need to get more information. For example, if Tess weren't sure what the GPA requirements were for the colleges she was interested in, she might need to look that up.

You can download a worksheet for this— Evidence For and Against, for Generalized Anxiety at http://www .newharbinger.com/32431.

Focused Attention

Your monkey mind is used to getting all your attention. The constant stream of chatter is so compelling that unless you focus your attention elsewhere you will be continually under its spell.

Imagine yourself sitting by a stream of monkey chatter. You could easily be totally absorbed in all the anxious thoughts bubbling up in front of you, but instead you close your eyes and focus inward on your breath. As you breathe in, notice the sensation and temperature of the air flowing in. As you breathe out, notice that. The breath itself is not what is important. What matters is that you are directing your attention away from your monkey's anxious thoughts.

You can do this anytime, whether you are worrying or not. In fact, training yourself how to *focus attention* when you are not worried is the best way to prepare for when you are.

Focusing your attention away from your monkey is powerful because it places you in the *present moment,* where your monkey cannot actually go. The monkey spends all its time reviewing the past, looking for mistakes you made, and imagining the future, looking for threats. No matter how many times you are distracted by anxious monkey chatter, just continue to bring your attention back to the present moment. This will help you find peace from worry and tame your monkey.

> *After using her taming tools for a while, Tess started to see her worries in a different light. She knew that getting less than a perfect grade would not lead directly to being "homeless and alone." Things were looking up!*

Tools to Rule the Generalized Anxiety Monkey

Spotting monkey chatter and coming up with your own alternative thoughts is essential to mastering generalized anxiety. But as long as you are still using avoidant behaviors like seeking reassurance, making too many lists, studying too hard, or just plain worrying, you are playing by your monkey's rules.

When you respond to monkey chatter by worrying, you are saying, *You are right, monkey. This is something I need to worry about.* You are giving your monkey a banana—training it to view the imagined threat as a real one and allowing it to continue to run your life.

To rule the monkey mind, you have to stop the avoidance cycle. Here's a powerful tool to help you on your way.

Worry Time

Your experience with worrying up until now has been monkey driven. That is, whenever your monkey chatters, you worry. You may not want to stop whatever you are doing at that moment and begin to worry, but you have no choice. There is a wild little monkey in charge.

During *worry time*, you are in charge—not your monkey. You decide when to worry and for how long. That's right—you are going to worry *on purpose*. You are going to worry good and hard, doing nothing else but worrying, for the ten- to twenty-minute duration of this exercise.

Your worry time should be planned in advance, so you will need to look at your day and decide on a time. It can be helpful to schedule it soon before something that you look forward to—such as calling a friend, going on your computer, or watching a movie. The reason for this is that you will never *feel* like spending time worrying. Worry time won't be fun, but it will change your relationship to worry in a good way!

When your scheduled worry time arrives, find a quiet place where you won't be disturbed, set a timer, take your top worries, and let them rip. Don't stop until the timer goes off.

Here is a script of Tess's worry time:

I got a B on the test. Oh, this is terrible! This B could ruin my life! It might affect my overall GPA, and that would be a disaster. I may not get into any good colleges because of this. I am also embarrassed I got a B. What if my friends start thinking that I'm not that smart? That would be terrible. But what is really awful about this is that if I can't get into a good college my whole life will be bad. I may not be able to get a good job. My life will be ruined if I can't get a good job. I may never be able to support myself!

When you worry as hard as you can, there are a few things that might happen: You might become very anxious, which is just fine. This is the time for it. Imagine yourself putting out a welcome mat during worry time, welcoming in all the anxious thoughts and as much anxiety as possible, without putting up any resistance.

If you begin to feel overwhelmed by fear, shift your attention away from the worry and focus on the bodily sensation that the worry causes. Breathe into that sensation, relaxing your belly. Remember that your breath is always there when you need it. (For more on breathing into anxiety, go back and revisit chapter 5.)

Another thing that can happen is that your mind may wander away from your worries. Worrying may become boring. This, too, is fine, so long as you bring your mind back to your worries. This may happen over and over again, but that's okay. The more often you direct your thoughts back to your worries, the better. This is what worry time is for.

The best thing about doing this exercise regularly is that whenever your monkey mind starts to chatter noisily throughout the day, you can tell it firmly that you will give it your full attention, but only during worry time. Do your best to continue to do whatever you are doing in that moment, other than worrying. You can even write the worry thought down so that you don't forget what to worry about during your worry time.

Remember that worry time, like all endeavors, takes discipline. You will need to commit to a time every day and follow through. And you may need

many sessions before you notice a change. But with practice you will find yourself more and more in charge, and your monkey will become easier to ignore. By taking control of when and how to worry, you are depriving your monkey of its usual reward. *No banana today, sorry!* This is how you tame the little critter.

You can download a Worry Time worksheet at http://www. newharbinger.com/32431.

The Relaxation Response

Generalized worry can cause a lot of stress in the body. Every time you treat monkey chatter as a signal of real danger, you trigger a fight-or-flight response.

When the fight-or-flight response is activated your heart beats faster, your muscles tense up, and your stomach stops digesting so that more energy can go to your large muscles. This would be fine if you were actually using your body to outrun a saber-toothed tiger or protect yourself against a bully. But the things that teens with generalized anxiety worry about are not things that will put them in immediate danger. You don't use your large muscles to fight or run from these things, so you don't get any release.

Constant worrying and the fight-or-flight response create a lot of muscle tension that can cause headaches and body aches. Your stomach may be in knots, causing stomachaches or diarrhea. Your heart beating faster than it needs to and your body being on high alert create nervous exhaustion. You may feel tired all the time and also have difficulty falling asleep.

Have you ever watched a cat when it catches sight of a dog? The cat arches its back, its fur stands on end, and it hisses. As soon as the dog is out of sight, the cat lies back down in the sun, stretching out its arms and legs, and purrs.

What the cat has done, naturally and automatically, is normalized itself after a threat has passed. When the dog

165

appeared, the fight-or-flight response was activated. The dog disappeared and something else was activated. It's called the *relaxation response.* It is as powerful as the fight-or-flight response, and as necessary.

If it were possible for a cat to have generalized anxiety, it would not stretch back out and purr after the dog left. Instead it would be constantly anticipating the next dog that might come along. It would be like you, always in a state of worry and tension, and it would not be able to relax.

Fortunately, you have the relaxation response too. It doesn't get activated like it should, because your worries are always triggering the fight-or-flight response. But you can train your body to activate this response and learn to truly relax.

The Golden Ball

To do this exercise, you need to sit or lie down for ten minutes with no distractions. So find a private place and turn your phone off.

Begin by closing your eyes and breathing slowly through your nose. Inhale deep down into your belly, and when you exhale say the word *relax*, or some other word or phrase that represents relaxation to you—such as *peace* or *let go* or *it's okay*. Do this ten times.

Now imagine that there is a golden ball of light over your head. This ball opens up and slowly pours its shimmering golden contents down over you, bathing your forehead, your eyes, and your jaw. It's like warm honey that melts the tension in your neck, shoulders, and chest.

As you inhale, slowly draw the golden light down deep into your belly. As you exhale, keep repeating your relaxation word or phrase. Let the warm, golden light radiate down into your hips, your thighs, your knees, your calves—all the way to your toes.

It is very likely that while you are doing this exercise your monkey mind will continue to do its job, bringing up worries that draw your attention. This is perfectly all right. When you notice an anxious thought has distracted you, say, *Thank you, monkey*, then bring your attention back to your breath and to whatever part of your body the warm golden light was on.

You may find it helpful to listen to music during this exercise. You can download an audio track with guided instructions at http://www.newharbinger.com/32431.

To get noticeable benefit from this relaxation technique, you will need to do it a minimum of once a day for six weeks.

You will get even better results if you do it twice a day. This may seem like a lot of time, but if you compare the few minutes a day these exercises would take to all the time you spend worrying, it won't seem so bad.

> *Tess got a B on her test, which wasn't as good as she had hoped. She was disappointed, but because she'd been using her taming tools regularly, she did not go back to worrying about getting into a good college. She was able to put her attention into learning the new material she was getting in the class. She knew that, besides being prepared by studying, there was nothing else she could do. Her grades were up to her teacher, and beyond her control.*

When you welcome the anxiety of not knowing how everything will turn out, you stop the avoidance cycle. Monkey miscalculations have turned your life into a minefield, where everything you want to do has to be agonized over. You deserve much more. You deserve to live the life you envision for yourself, free of senseless worry. What are you waiting for?

Chapter 10

Separation Anxiety

Stand by Me

Maria hated to be alone. It was worse at night, but she did not like to be alone during the day either. She had been dating her boyfriend, Roberto, for six months and was in almost constant contact with him, texting and calling him at all hours. If he did not respond immediately she began to panic, worrying that something had happened to him. What if he was in an accident? *Maria wondered.* Or what if he's no longer interested in me? *So she texted and called Roberto repeatedly until he responded. When he told her that he felt suffocated by her, Maria felt even more anxious and began checking on Roberto even more frequently, even though she knew it was pushing him away.*

Maria has *separation anxiety,* the fear of being away from a person one feels particularly attached to. If you have separation anxiety, you may feel closely attached to a parent, a close friend, or someone you are dating. When you're separated from this person, even for a few hours, you begin to feel anxious or on edge. You feel as if you will be alone forever, the person may die or leave for good, and you will fall apart.

As you have learned in this book, anxiety is triggered by anxious thoughts. These anxious thoughts are generated by the part of our brain most devoted to keeping us safe—the part we call the monkey mind. Your monkey takes its job very seriously. When you look at the experience of being separated from a parent or a loved one through the eyes of a hypervigilant monkey, whose total focus is keeping you protected and safe, you can see where those anxious thoughts come from.

We are all born dependent on our parents or caregivers. As babies we cannot care for ourselves. If no one responded to our cries, we would die. As infants, we will respond to anyone who will care for us, but we learn to recognize our parents or caregivers very early on and grow attached to them, just as the parents grow attached to the infant.

At around nine months of age, a child may cry or scream if her caretaker leaves the room or if a stranger tries to pick her up. This dependence on the caregiver is adaptive. It keeps the toddler from going too far away from the parent she depends on to feed her and keep her safe. By the age of two, when children are walking and ready for more independence, they understand that the parent will return.

So what about Maria's dependence on her boyfriend? You and I, and even Maria, can see that her anxiety is not rooted in reality. Maria is not dependent on Roberto for food and care. Maria's monkey mind is making miscalculations that are triggering her to act in a way that is not in her best interest. Instead of growing closer to the boy she loves, she's pushing him away.

Maria's monkey is sounding a full-scale alarm in a situation that is not actually dangerous. It is making the classic mistake it makes in all types of anxiety: over/underestimating. It is overestimating the chance that Roberto's goodbye is forever—that she will never see him again—and it is underestimating her ability to be alone.

Maria's monkey mind has convinced her that she must act on her anxious feelings by avoiding being alone. When she checks to make sure Roberto is still alive and hasn't left her, Maria is avoiding what it feels like to *not know*. That, for Maria, is a very scary feeling. When Roberto is not with her, Maria begins to feel like a baby whose parent has left the room.

Of course, Roberto is still alive. And he hasn't been driven so crazy by her constant checking up on him that he has broken up with her, so sooner or later he does return to her. And guess who gets the credit for that?

Monkey thought: *Roberto has not responded to your text. Maybe he wants to break up with you!*

Avoidant behavior: Text or call Roberto to check on him. Ask him if he wants to break up with you.

Monkey logic: *Because you checked up on him, Roberto is staying with you.*

Monkey thought: *Roberto is flying to visit his grandparents in Arizona. He may die on the plane and you will never see him again!*

Avoidant behavior: Try to convince him not to go, or to drive instead of fly, or to let you go with him.

Monkey logic: *Because he drove instead of flying, or because you were with him, he didn't die.*

Monkey thought: *If you are alone you will feel panicky, and you can't stand that feeling!*

Avoidant behavior: Talk with friends on Facebook or by text. Get someone to hang out with you.

Monkey logic: *Because you were connected with other people, you did not panic or completely lose control.*

Maria doesn't like her monkey's chatter and would like it to quiet down, but the only way she knows to shut her monkey up is to follow its instructions: *Avoid being alone. Phone or text Roberto now!* While this relieves her anxiety and quiets her monkey for a little while, in the long run it makes her monkey louder and her separation anxiety worse.

Every time Maria avoids her aloneness by texting or phoning Roberto, and then Roberto returns to her, Maria's monkey gets a banana. Why? She is rewarding her monkey's logic that avoiding being alone is what saved her. The scary chatter gets louder and it seems more urgent, and Maria's world gets smaller and smaller.

What are you avoiding to keep your monkey mind quiet? Here are some common avoidant behaviors of teens with separation anxiety.

- Avoiding going far away from home or the person you are attached to. This may mean avoiding trips with family or friends, or avoiding overnight school field trips.

- Doing things with the person you are attached to, not because you want to do those things but because you are avoiding being apart.

- Avoiding ever being alone. You may plan your days according to what will keep you around people, as opposed to how you really want to spend time.

- Avoiding doing things with friends, because you are so worried when you are away from the person you are attached to.

Tools to Tame the Separation Anxiety Monkey

If you have separation anxiety, chances are that the anxious thoughts driving your behavior are unconscious. You have been acting on them so long that they are automatic. You don't question them or look at their origin. As long as these thoughts remain in the dark, you will keep acting on them. The first step to reducing anxiety's hold on you is to use your taming tools to shine some light on these anxious thoughts.

Spot the Thought

Think of a recent situation that made you anxious. Ask yourself these two questions:

1. *What am I afraid of?*

2. *What is the worst thing that could happen if this were true?*

These are the thoughts that drove your behavior in that situation. Understand that monkey thoughts may be very scary and believable to you, but they are not realistic assessments of risk. In fact, that's how you will recognize them—by their miscalculations! Monkeys can't calculate the actual odds of something happening. A monkey thought is at best a wild guess, always slanted toward perceiving danger and keeping you safe.

You can download a Spot the Thought worksheet at http://www.newharbinger.com/32431.

Monkey Miscalculations

Besides the over/underestimating mistake, the two most common monkey miscalculations that occur with separation anxiety are catastrophizing and intolerance of uncertainty. Here's what they look like.

Catastrophizing

To the monkey mind, goodbyes are forever. A loved one who leaves may never return. And being alone is the worst thing in the world—causing panic and loss of control.

Of course, being alone for a while is not a catastrophe. You've survived without this person in the past. And even if the worst happened, and you did not ever see the person again, you would learn to live without that person. But when your monkey has you convinced you are in a catastrophic emergency situation, you forget all that.

Here are some examples of this monkey miscalculation:

- *If the person is far away, she is much more likely to die.*

- *If you have not heard from her in the past few minutes or hours, she may be hurt or dead.*

- *If she is late meeting you, she may be dead or injured.*

- *If she is around other people, she may fall out of love with you and in love with someone else.*

- *If you hear a siren, it might be for her.*

If you suspect your monkey is catastrophizing, ask yourself, *What is a more likely explanation?*

Intolerance of Uncertainty

The monkey mind cannot stand not knowing what the outcome will be in any situation. It must be absolutely 100 percent certain that you will be safe and everything will be okay. The truth is that we can never know that everything will be okay. When you take this monkey miscalculation seriously, you are attempting to achieve the impossible.

Ask yourself, *What cost am I paying by trying to eliminate all risk from my relationship?*

Alternative Thoughts

With all anxiety problems, the monkey mind is doing all of the thinking, and with all of its miscalculations it is obvious that thinking is not what the monkey mind is good at. Your monkey's great skill is looking for and reacting to threats that could hurt you. If you have separation anxiety your monkey mind is hyperactive, jumping up and down, yelling one "what if" after the other: *What if this happens?! What if that?!*

In order to stop the avoidance cycle that keeps your separation anxiety going, you'll need to begin asking *What else? What else is more likely to be true?* You can see alternatives that your monkey cannot.

Here are some of the alternative thoughts Maria came up with:

Situation: Roberto said he would call me at nine. When he didn't call, I texted him but he didn't respond.

Monkey "what if?" thought: *What if he met someone else and he's breaking up with me?*

Monkey miscalculation: Catastrophizing

Alternative thought: *It is more likely that he is not responding to my texts because they annoy him, not because he is breaking up with me.*

Situation: Roberto is flying to Arizona.

Monkey "what if?" thought: *What if the plane crashes and he dies?*

Monkey miscalculation: Intolerance of uncertainty

Alternative thought: *I can take this chance. I don't need to go with him or ask him not to go just because I am afraid.*

Once Maria came up with some alternative thoughts, her feelings did not go away but they weren't quite as overwhelming. Having alternative thoughts helped her gain some distance from her monkey mind, and this is a very important first step. Take the time right now to come up with some alternative thoughts to your own monkey chatter. Changing your thinking is the best way to prepare yourself for what comes next: changing your behavior. Download an Alternative Thoughts worksheet at http://www.newharbinger .com/32431.

Tools to Rule the Separation Anxiety Monkey

Are you ready to stop following your monkey's rules and start following your own? It's easier to say than to do. You will need to give up the avoidant behaviors you've been using to keep from facing the separation you fear. This is going to make you feel a lot more anxious in the short run. Ruling your monkey takes tremendous courage and commitment. Is it worth it to you?

Life Compass

To answer this question, try another paper and pencil exercise. Write down the behaviors your monkey has gotten you to do in order to manage your separation anxiety. Are these behaviors working for you?

Next, write down all the things that you would like to be able to do. Are any of these things worth fighting for?

Here is what Maria came up with:

1. Let him call me instead of me being the one to call him all the time.

2. Hang out with my girlfriends or go ice-skating instead of obsessing about where he is.

3. I would like to bring up my grades, which means studying more instead of obsessing about him.

Writing these things down was like holding a life compass. It told Maria which direction she needed to go, her true north. She'd been going south with her monkey long enough. In her heart she felt she had the courage to follow her life compass instead.

Do you have goals that are important enough to fight for? If you do, keep reading. Facing your fears and changing your behaviors are extremely powerful ways to get your life back. But like most things worth fighting for, it is hard work.

You can download a Life Compass worksheet at http://www.newharbinger.com/32431.

Worst-Case Scenario

Roll up your sleeves and ready yourself for the first piece of hard work: imagining the worst. That's right, your task is to close your eyes and imagine the very worst thing that could happen in regard to the person or people you are attached to.

You may be thinking, *That certainly is not going to help! I imagine the worst all the time. That's why I keep texting him or calling her, to make certain the worst has not happened!*

The thing is, every time you act on an anxious monkey thought by making certain the worst has not happened, your monkey wins. You are, in effect, saying that the thought is important, and something must be done. You are agreeing with your monkey's catastrophizing. You are saying you cannot tolerate uncertainty. You're saying, *You're absolutely right, monkey!* and giving it a banana.

To stop the avoidance cycle you need to imagine the worst—your boyfriend is injured or dead, your girlfriend hates you, whatever sounds the most terrible to you—and accept it. Don't act on it. Don't check. Simply be alone with an idea that terrifies you.

In this exercise you won't be following your monkey's script. You will be the director, not your monkey. You are going to write out an imaginary scenario of what you are most afraid of, a real horror movie. You'll want lots of gory details in this script because the whole point is to get as anxious as possible. To make it sound real, write it in the present tense. For example, you could begin with, *I am waiting for my mother to pick me up at school and I hear a siren in the distance…*

Of course this is just the beginning. Ask yourself what is the worst it could mean if your mother is late picking you up. This helps you get to the core fear—for example, that she has forgotten you and you will be standing in front of your school until nighttime, or that she has gotten in a car accident and is in the hospital or is dead. That's the sort of worst-case scenario you need.

Here is what Maria's scenario looked like:

Roberto has not responded to my texts! My heart is beating fast and my hands are feeling sweaty. I can feel that something is not right. I text him that I am really worried and to please let me know he is okay, but he still doesn't text me back. Each minute that goes by feels like an hour. He is not responding! I know he was riding with friends and they were driving too fast and they were in a car accident. He's lying in the street right now, bleeding and broken with nobody there to help. His cell phone is lying right next to him with all my texts, but he is in too much pain to pick it up. Tears are coming to my eyes thinking about this. He's going to die and there is nothing that I can do. I'll never see him again! My life will be ruined! I will never, ever get over this loss!

Maria did a great job, didn't she? Many people have difficulty thinking about disastrous situations, especially when they involve harm to loved ones. The whole reason you've been seeking reassurance from your loved ones is to avoid thinking those kinds of thoughts.

Be assured that imagining terrible scenes for the purpose of confronting your fears is in no way the same thing as wanting it to happen. We are taught that imagining things—in the form of positive affirmations and prayer, for example—can make them come true. But there is no way that picturing things you feel could happen—whether you want them to or not—can make them come true.

What you are going to do with your own worst-case scenario is write it out—perhaps with the worksheet available at http://www.newharbinger.com/32431—and read it to yourself, over and over. You can even record it on your cell phone or computer so you can play it to yourself too. You are going to treat this scenario as if it were medicine you had to take regularly to stay alive. Carve out twenty minutes a day, every day, to read it or listen to it over and over.

It is important that you do this with the right attitude. You are to accept whatever feelings come up in you and welcome them with your breath. (Reread the section on the "welcoming breath" in chapter 5.)

The idea is to focus your attention on breathing into wherever the sensation is the strongest. If your stomach is clenching, your shoulders are tense, or your hands are shaking or sweating, imagine that as you inhale, you are breathing down into that part of your body, making room for the anxious sensations.

The point is not to relax while you do this—quite the opposite. You are allowing yourself to feel the anxiety, and you are surrendering to it. By welcoming the feelings, you are teaching your mind and body that these monkey thoughts are something that you are willing to face, and by doing this you will be taking back control. You are no longer playing by your monkey's rules. You are playing by your own.

In a horror movie, when you come to the part where the bad guy is about to kill a bunch of unsuspecting teens in a cabin, you may feel really, really scared, to the point that you want to scream. But you don't get up and call 911, because you know it is a movie—it is not really happening. If you were to keep watching that horrible part of the movie over and over again, by the fiftieth viewing (or probably much sooner) you would not feel scared at all.

You would not get used to it if you were to keep your eyes closed partway while watching it over and over again. In order to get used to something, you have to open your eyes and let yourself see it all. It is the same with your anxious monkey thoughts. If you keep thinking them on purpose, they lose their power. The less you do to try to control the thought, and the more you welcome it, the less anxiety it will bring.

When you face something that is not truly dangerous, whether it is a movie scene or your own anxious thoughts and feelings, you will get used to it and know that you do not need to act on it at all.

The worst-case scenario exercise is important practice for what comes next, so don't take it lightly. When you've reread your script so many times that it seems almost silly, you'll know you are in charge. You'll be ready to change your behavior.

The Challenge Ladder

Avoidant behaviors—like never allowing yourself to be alone, going places you don't want to go to just to be near someone, and checking to make sure that person is alive—are what have been feeding your monkey, making your separation anxiety stronger and stronger. You will change these behaviors one at a time, starting with the least scary situations and moving up slowly, like climbing rungs on a ladder. (Download the Challenge Ladder worksheet at http://www.newharbinger.com/32431.)

You can make different rungs on your ladder by varying the distance and time out of contact with the person you are dependent on. Here is what Maria's ladder looked like:

Go away for a weekend without Roberto and only call or text him once each day

Sleepover with friends while Roberto is away for a weekend and only call or text him once

Take a walk around neighborhood alone without my phone

1 hour in room studying without talking to anyone using phone or computer

1 day without texting or calling Roberto; phone on for incoming calls and texts only

4 hours no texting or calling Roberto; phone on for incoming calls and texts only

Turn phone off 1 hour; no texting or calling Roberto

Turn phone off 30 minutes; no texting or calling Roberto

By not checking up on Roberto constantly, Maria realized, she would have extra time to herself to fill. To help her focus on other things besides Roberto while she worked up the rungs of her ladder, she made a short list of things she used to do. They included studying, listening to music, talking with or doing things with friends, and going to the ice skating rink.

When Maria started on the first rung, the first fifteen minutes went by pretty easily, but it wasn't long before she began to feel bored and agitated. She felt the urge to pick up her phone to see if Roberto had called her, just as she had done so many times in the past. Her monkey had gotten her in a habit of checking her phone every few minutes, and not doing so felt strange.

This was a good sign that Maria was on the right track. Feeling strange is good. If the exercise is comfortable for you, either you are not doing it right, or you picked something that is too easy for you—in which case you should go to the next rung on your ladder.

By the time her first half hour was up, Maria couldn't wait to call Roberto and tell him what she had just done. He didn't seem very impressed, and he suggested she try not calling for a longer period. Maria knew she wasn't ready for that. For the next few days she repeated her half-hour exercise several times a day, and by the fifth time she noticed it was easy. Her monkey mind was still chattering away, telling her to call Roberto, but somehow it didn't seem that compelling. And she was actually finding some of her English assignments interesting. She found herself thinking, I can do this! *It was time to move up another rung.*

Within a few weeks, Maria could go all morning without calling or texting Roberto. She took regular walks around her neighborhood without her cell phone, and she could study for an hour at a stretch without being too distracted by monkey alarms. The thought of doing an overnight without checking on her boyfriend still sounded like too much for her, so she kept working the rung below it, building up courage. When he went away with his grandparents, she called him more than she had planned, but less than she used to.

Over time, it became easier and easier for Maria to go longer periods without checking on Roberto. Although her monkey mind kept coming up with thoughts that her boyfriend was injured or dead, or had left her, and that she would never see him again, her alternative thoughts that he was safe and still loved her felt more true. She had so much more time in her life now for other things in addition to Roberto. And then something else happened that really surprised her. In the past Roberto almost never called her or texted her, and he ignored most of her checks on him. Now he was calling and texting her as much as she was calling and texting him! She realized that following her monkey's rules had been having the effect of pushing Roberto away. Now that she was in charge, not only was she was becoming more independent but she and Roberto were growing closer together.

Are you ready to rule your separation anxiety monkey? There is nothing holding you back from being truly independent except your own anxious thoughts and feelings. Healthy relationships depend on you being comfortable being alone, able to stand on your own two feet. Have courage—you can do it!

Chapter 11

Obsessive-Compulsive Disorder

Don't Step on That Crack!

Jon was super excited to be a newly licensed driver. A week into his independence there was a tragic accident in his town, in which another teenager hit and killed a pedestrian crossing the street. The next time Jon was driving he felt a slight bump in the road. The thought popped into his head that maybe he had just run over somebody. He knew this was ridiculous, but he could not get this fear out of his head. Even though he didn't see anything when he checked his rearview mirror, he still felt anxious. It was not until he circled back around to the spot where he'd felt the bump and saw that there was nothing there that his anxiety decreased.

Ever since seventh-grade health education class, when homosexuality was discussed, Dan noticed the thought What if I am gay? *popping into his head. He was attracted to girls, and had nothing against gay people. (In fact, his best friend had two moms.) But this doubt caused him considerable anxiety. All sorts of things started to trigger the thought. Seeing male models in magazines, any words for homosexuality, even being around girls would trigger the thought. He began to mentally reassure himself with evidence that he was not gay. He monitored his body closely for any signs of arousal when around males. Doing so made him feel a little better for a short while, but the doubt just wouldn't go away.*

Shaneesha first started washing her hands when she was around anyone who was sick. She had thought this was reasonable because her frail grandmother lived with her and everyone in the family took precautions to prevent her from getting sick. Then Shaneesha had the thought that her clothes may have come into contact with germs that were on school desks or any public place. She began to change her clothes as soon as she got home. This helped reduce her anxiety at first, but then she felt she needed to change her clothes and take a shower, and after that not come into contact with anything that could have gotten contaminated at school—including her phone, backpack, or books. She knew this had gone too far, but the feelings were so strong she couldn't stop herself.

Lucia was known in her family as a perfectionist. Her room was always neat, her books and papers organized, her clothes color-coded in her closet. She liked it this way and it did not cause a problem. But for no apparent reason, things started to get out of control. While doing assigned reading, she started to doubt that she fully understood what she had just read, so she began to reread everything. She started erasing and rewriting portions of her reports that didn't look just right to her. She worried she may have left an important assignment behind in her classroom, locker, or car, so she went back and checked over and over again. She checked her backpack repeatedly to make sure she had everything in it. This checking began to take up a lot of time and was frustrating and stressful to her, but Lucia had trouble resisting the urge.

T hese four teens all suffer from obsessive-compulsive disorder, or OCD. Unlike the other types of anxiety in this book, OCD behavior can vary a great deal from teen to teen, which can make things a little confusing. But once we define OCD "obsessions" and "compulsions" you will see how they are all the same problem.

Obsessions

We often speak of being obsessed with a song, a sports team, or another person. Though we may not be able to get our minds off of those things, they are fun to think about. This is never the case with OCD obsessions.

OCD obsessions are intrusive thoughts, images, or urges that you do not want and that cause you anxiety and distress. Even though these thoughts originate in your own head, they make little rational sense. Obsessive thoughts are generated in the part of your brain that is totally devoted to detecting threats—the monkey mind, where making wild guesses is standard operating procedure.

OCD obsessions are also different from other kinds of worries because of their content. General worries, such as those discussed in the chapter on generalized anxiety, are about everyday types of things, like grades, money, and other people. OCD obsessions tend to be a little strange—like wondering if you ran someone over, thinking about hurting yourself or others, being concerned about germs on your clothes, needing things arranged just right, or doubting your own sexual orientation. If you have these kinds of obsessions, you know they are odd and you may be too embarrassed to talk about them with your friends.

Most obsessions fall into one of four categories:

Contamination: thinking you will "catch something" or be poisoned by touching a surface or object (or less commonly, fears of being contaminated by people with disabilities or unlikable characteristics, as if being around them or even thinking about them can make you become like them)

- Concern about germs and diseases, such as sexually transmitted infections, stomach flu, or cancer

- Fear of coming into contact with bodily fluids, like urine or feces

- Worrying about possible poisoning from common household cleaners like bleach and pesticides, or things in the environment, like radiation or poisonous plants

Harm or aggression: thinking that you caused, or will cause, physical or emotional harm to someone else or to yourself

- Worrying that by doing something—or forgetting to do something—you will cause a fire, flood, burglary, or similar disaster

- Fear that you might do something like stab someone, run someone over, trip an old person, or say a random and hurtful thing

- Fear of not being careful enough and causing an injury by slipping or stepping on something, or ingesting something bad—like pills left out or spoiled food

Forbidden sexual or religious thoughts: thoughts that undermine your identity or your sense of being a good or decent person

- Doubts about your sexual orientation

- Thoughts about being a child molester or committing incest

- Thoughts about sex with someone forbidden, like a teacher

- Thoughts about aggressive sexual acts, such as rape

- Thoughts about saying something against God

- Excessive concern with what is right and wrong or moral and immoral

Symmetry or exactness: having a general sense of discomfort unless things are "just so," or done in a certain way—or if something seems unfinished

- Needing things to be even, exact, or perfectly balanced

- Worrying about forgetting or losing something important

- Needing to know or remember things

- Having difficulty making decisions or throwing things away

If your obsessive thoughts don't quite fit into one of these four categories, that doesn't mean you don't have OCD. The defining feature of OCD is intrusive thoughts that cause anxiety. That's where the other half of OCD—the compulsions—comes in.

Compulsions

OCD compulsions are behaviors with strict rules that you feel you must follow in order to prevent the things you're obsessively thinking about from actually happening. These behaviors are considered compulsive due to the strong urge the OCD sufferer feels to do them. They are different from a normal routine in that they take up more time than you would like them to. Here are some common compulsions:

Checking

- Checking to make sure you didn't make a mistake

- Checking that you didn't forget something or leave something behind

- Checking that you did not or will not cause harm

- Checking that you unplugged appliances or turned them off

- Checking to make sure you didn't drop something

- Checking that you didn't run someone over while driving

197

- Seeking reassurance from others that you didn't do something bad or hurt someone, or that they are not sick, or that something is clean

Cleaning and washing

- Hand washing or showering a certain way, length of time, or number of times

- Excessively washing your clothes or other belongings

- Washing yourself more than ordinarily necessary after going to the bathroom

- Doing other things—like wiping your hands or using hand sanitizer—to get rid of possible contaminants

Mental compulsions

- Making mental lists, or reviewing things in your mind

- Using special words, images, or numbers (sometimes in response to a "bad" thought or image)

- Saying prayers in a set way to prevent something bad from happening

- Counting in your head while doing something a "right" or "safe" or "good" number of times

Repeating

- Touching, tapping, or rubbing things in a certain way or a certain number of times, or turning things on and off again

- Doing things over again—like going in and out of doorways, getting up and down in chairs, or getting in and out of cars

- Repeating body movements like blinking

- Rereading, erasing, and rewriting; reviewing things in your mind that you may have said or done

Ordering or arranging

- Lining things up or ordering and arranging your belongings so that things seem just right (for example, having your clothes color-coded, things lined up at right angles, or your desk arranged in a certain way)

Once again, if you have a compulsion that doesn't quite fit one of these descriptions, it does not mean you don't have OCD. Your obsessions and compulsions, while seeming pretty strange, do stem from the same thing all anxiety problems stem from—the desire to keep yourself safe. Your monkey mind is just trying to do its job of keeping you alive. It's doing what it does best: sensing danger, even where there is none, and sounding the alarm to tell you *Be afraid—very afraid!*

But what are you actually afraid of? Why are OCD obsessions so powerful—powerful enough to make you act out compulsions over and over throughout your day?

What's Going On?

Although the content of your obsession may not sound like life or death to others, or even to yourself—*Will I really burn down the house if I don't check for the third time that the iron is turned off?*—your body is nevertheless in fight-or-flight mode. How do little ideas trigger such big fears?

Everyone has scary, intrusive thoughts—not just people with OCD. The brain is like a popcorn machine, churning out all sorts of thoughts, estimated by some neuroscientists to be as many as fifty thousand a day. Among all this popping there are some pretty weird and scary thoughts. In fact, probably about half of the thoughts that get popped on a daily basis are in the unpleasant category, having to do with how something could go wrong.

If your monkey mind is hardwired to be extra sensitive to threat, it will view these thoughts as evidence that there is something wrong and you are in danger. Suddenly, what was a random piece of popcorn becomes a killer kernel and your monkey sounds the alarm.

Monkey Miscalculations

No matter how horrific, how crazy, how embarrassing and shameful your obsessive thought may be, the thought is not the problem. Your interpretation of the thought is what gives it power. To your monkey, your having that thought means that something is wrong with you, that you might act on that thought, or that you must do something to prevent that thought from coming true. It makes the classic over/under monkey miscalculation.

1. It overestimates the threat that something terrible will happen to you or someone you love, or that you will actually act on a destructive thought that you have.

2. It underestimates your ability to tolerate the anxiety or discomfort that you will feel if you do not do your compulsions, as well as your ability to cope if something bad actually does happen.

The other monkey miscalculation that matters with OCD is *intolerance of uncertainty*. Even if there is a 1 percent chance that something could go wrong, you should try to prevent it. When you do a compulsion to make things safe, doubt creeps in. No matter how far you go to make things absolutely 100 percent safe, the monkey mind will doubt whether you have done enough. There is simply no amount of risk that is acceptable to the monkey mind. With OCD you can never know you are safe.

-   You washed your hands, but then you touched the faucet. Your monkey says, *Others with dirty hands have touched that faucet! You should wash your hands again.*

- You unplugged the curling iron. Your monkey says, *But what if you unplugged something else instead? You should go back and check.*

- You know you are attracted to the opposite sex, but you happened to have the thought that you might be gay. Your monkey says, *You need to think about this to figure it out.*

- You said goodnight to your parents, but you got interrupted. The monkey mind says, *If you don't get it right, something bad could happen to them. Say it again.*

Once you've spotted your OCD monkey and its miscalculations, I'm not going to encourage you to come up with alternative thoughts as we do with other types of anxiety. The reason for this is that no matter how accurate an alternative thought might be, your monkey mind will cast doubt on it. With OCD your monkey's intolerance of uncertainty is so high that it will cast doubt on your alternative thoughts too.

The OCD Avoidance Cycle

Random anxious thoughts become obsessive thoughts only when the monkey mind interprets them as important. When it sounds the alarm and you are flooded with anxiety, you do what everyone with anxiety tries to do—avoid it.

That's where your compulsions come in. To get some relief from the anxiety, you perform little rituals that either distract you from the terrible thought or give you the illusion that you are preventing it from coming true. If your obsession is around a fear of germs, washing your hands eases the anxiety. The obsession loses its hold on you and you can relax. If that were the end of it, life would be easy.

The problem is that avoiding anxiety is always, at best, a short-term solution. While you get a few minutes of relief, you are only postponing the pain and ultimately making it worse. Why? Because of monkey logic.

When your monkey sees you washing your hands it says, *I was right; those germs I warned you about* are *dangerous.* When your monkey sees your relief after you wash your hands it says, *You washed your hands and you are relieved. Therefore washing your hands in the future will keep you relieved.* When your monkey sees you didn't get sick it says, *Because you washed your hands you didn't get sick.*

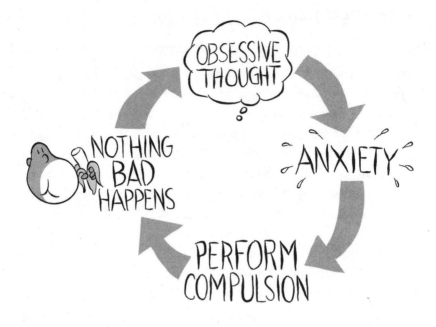

Here are some more examples of monkey logic at work with OCD:

Obsession: *What if I run over and kill someone?*

Compulsion or avoidance: Avoid busy intersections, and don't drive with music on. Check your rearview mirror or retrace your route to see if there are any bodies in the road.

Monkey logic: *Because you are extra careful and check your mirrors and routes, you have not hit anyone.*

Obsession: *What if I am gay and don't know it, and my whole life is a lie?*

Compulsion or avoidance: Reassure yourself that you have always been attracted to the opposite sex. Avoid looking at attractive people of the same sex or having any physical contact with them. Check your body for signs of arousal around them.

Monkey logic: *Because you mentally review the evidence that you're not gay, you can be certain that you're still straight.*

Obsession: *What if I bring home germs that could make me or people in my family sick?*

Compulsion or avoidance: Avoid touching things that other people have touched. When you have touched things in public places, wash your body, clothes, and belongings.

Monkey logic: *Because you are so careful with your washing rituals, no one in your family has gotten seriously ill.*

Obsession: *What if I were to forget something important and because of it I missed an assignment and got a bad grade If things are not just right, I might feel horrible forever.*

Compulsion or avoidance: Check your backpack repeatedly to make sure you haven't forgotten something or left something behind. Keep your room organized so that you can relax.

Monkey logic: *Because you check and recheck your backpack and keep your room organized, you don't forget anything and are safe.*

You cannot reason with the logic of the OCD monkey. It always says the same thing: *You are safe because you avoided thinking dangerous thoughts, and if you did think them, you did your compulsion to keep them from coming true.*

Every time you try not to think an obsessive thought you train your monkey that the thought is dangerous. You are telling it, *You are right to sound the alarm. I should not think terrible thoughts like that!* You are giving your monkey a banana.

Every time you perform a compulsion to keep an obsessive thought from coming true you are telling it, *Thanks for saving me from certain disaster, monkey!* Once again, you are giving it a banana.

This is why your obsessions get more powerful over time and your compulsions get increasingly complicated and time-consuming the more you use them. The only way to stop OCD from taking over your life is to start treating your obsessive thoughts as what they are—unimportant—and your compulsive rituals as what they are: unnecessary.

Tools to Rule the OCD Monkey

That's worth repeating. The only way to stop OCD from taking over your life is to start treating your obsessive thoughts as what they are—unimportant—and your compulsive rituals as what they are—unnecessary.

How can you treat your obsessive thoughts as unimportant? Simply by not avoiding them anymore, by exposing yourself to them.

You may say to yourself, *But I'm exposed to obsessive thoughts all the time. That's the problem!* This is not true. Since you've had no control of the thoughts themselves, you've been trying to avoid anything or any situation that might trigger the thoughts. And when that is not possible you have tried to get rid of the anxiety the thought caused by doing compulsions.

As you know, you cannot grit your teeth and will your anxious thoughts to go away. The harder you've tried, the more persistent they've become. That's because their power is fueled by your resistance to them. The more you resist them, the more convinced the monkey mind becomes that they are dangerous, and the more it will trigger alarms when you think them. Are you ready to try acceptance instead?

By accepting and welcoming obsessive thoughts, you prove to yourself that a thought is just a thought, no matter how horrifying it is. Accepting the obsessive thought means not performing compulsions to make it go away.

And what about the anxiety this will cause? Accept that too. Feel it. All the way to the end.

That's right, *to the end*. There is a beginning, a middle, and an end to every emotion, including anxiety. You've just never gotten past the beginning stage, in which you are doing everything you can to quash it.

Does that sound scary? It is. It is also incredibly powerful. Triggering your obsessive thoughts on purpose, and feeling the anxiety that comes when you don't act on your compulsion, is the most effective long-term treatment for OCD there is. It takes your monkey out of the process completely and puts you in charge. And if you don't rule your OCD monkey, it will continue to rule you!

Life Compass

Whenever your fight-or-flight response has been activated by obsessive thoughts, you've always taken flight. It's never worked very well, but it always seemed better than the alternative. This is the time to ask yourself what you are willing to fight for. What part of your life do you want back badly enough to face your worst fears?

It can be helpful to write down what OCD has taken away from you and how important these things are for you. Here is what Shaneesha came up with:

> I spend almost three hours a day washing and changing my clothes, time I'd rather spend with my friends, getting my homework done, or just relaxing.
>
> I avoid being around my grandmother, whom I love, because I'm so afraid of getting her sick.
> I want to be able to spend time with her again.
>
> My hands are chapped and look terrible, which is embarrassing to me. I want to have healthy hands and skin.

To help you identify what you have been avoiding because of your OCD, download the Life Compass worksheet at http://www.newharbinger.com/32431.

For Shaneesha it was no contest. Her compass pointed directly to her grandmother, whom she loved deeply. The idea that she could enjoy her grandmother's company without obsessing about germs and getting her sick sounded so sweet and so scary at the same time. In her heart, Shaneesha knew that if there were anything that could give her the courage she needed to try to beat her OCD, it would be her grandmother.

If you've used your compass and you know what your direction is, you know that what you've been doing in the past won't get you there. Avoiding obsessive thoughts doesn't work. They still pop up, and when they do pop up, avoiding the anxiety they bring by doing compulsions doesn't work for very long either.

Obsessive thoughts are only as powerful as you make them by resisting them. Are you ready to accept and welcome them instead?

Core Fear Scenario

On the surface, OCD obsessions can look deceptively silly, even to those suffering from them. But if you dig around a bit you'll find that underneath them lie deeper core fears. Unless you understand the core fear you'll never quite get over the scary thoughts on the surface. To help you uncover your core fear, here are three good questions to ask:

1. *What am I afraid will happen if I don't avoid my trigger and don't do any compulsions?*

2. *What is the worst thing that could happen?*

3. *What would this mean about me, my life, or my future?*

By way of example, here are Shaneesha's responses to them.

1. If I touch my backpack and don't wash my hands I might spread germs to my grandmother.

2. If I spread germs to my grandmother she might get sick and die because she is old and fragile.

3. If I were to spread germs to her and cause her to die, I would never be able to forgive myself, and others might blame me as well.

Once you have identified your core fear, grab a pen and paper because here you get a chance to get creative. You are going to write your *core fear scenario*. It's a description, written like a movie scene, that depicts in vivid detail what it would look like if your core fear came true. It should be as scary as possible—like a horror movie designed to make you, the audience, cringe. Download the Core Fear Scenario worksheet at http://www.newharbinger.com/32431.

You may balk at this at first. Most people with OCD have a very hard time exposing themselves to their obsessions, especially those that involve harm to loved ones—in Shaneesha's case, the idea of her grandmother dying. We have been taught that our thoughts are powerful and can influence outcomes. This is absolutely not the case with OCD.

Your obsessions are the result of a disorder, and you must treat them as such. Remember, the point of exposing yourself to your obsessions is so that these thoughts will lose some of their power. It is the same as if you decided to watch a horror movie over and over again. At first it would be really scary, but after the fiftieth time it would start to get boring. You need to learn to stop treating your thoughts as dangerous and avoiding them, because that will only fuel the disorder.

Here is Shaneesha's core fear scenario:

Because I have decided to face my OCD, I touch my backpack. I know my backpack has been on hundreds of different surfaces at school and in other places that are dirty and covered with germs. Now I have these dirty germs on my hands. My heart is already beating faster and I really want to wash my hands, but I don't. Instead I walk into my house and I begin touching things. I touch the door handle, the fridge handle, the countertops, and the dining room table. Now my heart is really beating and I feel hot and sweaty. I know my grandmother will come into contact with these surfaces. Then she will put her hands to her eyes, and the germs that I brought into the house will be in her body. I see her do this and I want to yell, "Stop! Don't touch your eyes!" But I don't. The next morning my grandmother comes to breakfast and she is coughing. This might be because I spread germs to her. By the end of the day she is really sick and has a fever, so my parents take her to the doctor. They end up hospitalizing her because she is so sick. I can't bring myself to visit her because this is probably all my fault. The next day my mother comes back and she is crying. She tells me that my grandmother has died. My heart sinks in my chest. I feel shame and sadness. My grandmother has died and it was my fault! My life will never be the same. I will never get over this!

Once you have written your core fear scenario, set aside at least a half hour (the longer the better) to read it to yourself repeatedly. You can also record the scenario on your phone or computer and play it back to yourself. After the first time you read or listen to it, write down how anxious it makes you feel using a number from 1 to 10, with 10 being the most anxious. Then keep reading or listening until either your anxiety comes down by 50 percent, or your time is up for that day.

Do this again the next day and every day thereafter, until the core fear scenario rates a one. This is a terrific preparation for the other half of welcoming your obsessions: not doing the compulsions that come along with them!

The Challenge Ladder

You'll be happy to know that I'm not going to ask you to confront every obsession and compulsion you have at once. Just as Justin did in chapter 4, it is best to make a ladder, welcoming one OCD situation at a time, beginning with the least scary. By way of example, let's look at how Shaneesha faced her fears, one rung at a time.

At the top of her ladder, Shaneesha put the thing in her life she was missing out on the most due to her OCD: being around her grandmother. She'd been protecting her grandmother from germs by compulsive washing, so she decided that the first rung on her ladder would be to touch her backpack and not wash her hands or use hand sanitizer. She would then touch surfaces in her home—doorknobs, tables, chairs, dishes, and pillows—that her monkey mind had previously designated as clean, and safe for grandmother to come into contact with.

Sound easy? To Shaneesha, doing this was very scary, but not impossible. It's important to begin with a challenge that is, with a little courage and good preparation, manageable. Download a Challenge Ladder worksheet at http://www .newharbinger.com/32431.

The moment Shaneesha touched her backpack she could feel the pangs of fear. She wanted to wash her hands so badly, but with the help of some deep breaths and some "Thank you, monkey"s she walked past the bathroom toward her grandmother's bedroom. Shaneesha's monkey howled its little head off, conjuring up images of her grandmother getting sick, on her deathbed, even at her funeral. Her monkey reminded her it would be all her fault and her whole family would blame her and her life would be ruined.

Shaneesha took a deep breath and touched her grandmother's doorknob. The fear felt like a punch in the stomach and her heart was beating wildly. It was all she could do to keep herself from running back to find her hand sanitizer. But she kept focusing on her breath and reminding herself that she was willing to take this risk. She knew that if she did not, her OCD monkey would continue to rule her life.

After a very uncomfortable half hour of touching various surfaces, Shaneesha noticed that her anxiety had decreased by about half, without her resorting to her usual compulsions! It seemed impossible, but it was true—her anxiety was coming down on its own. Every day for a week she repeated her experiment, and it became easier and easier. Not only was she feeling less anxious, but her obsessions became more and more ridiculous to her. Nothing terrible happened.

This experience gave Shaneesha confidence to continue up her ladder, until finally she got to the top rung: a trip to a hospital waiting room. She sat in a chair, read magazines, and touched things just as anyone would do. When she got home, she did wash her hands once quickly, but that seemed like what someone without OCD would do, and she did not change her clothing the whole rest of the day. She went to the waiting room six more times, and by the end of her practice she felt terrific! Her hands were no longer raw and chapped from constant washing. She was no longer wasting time and energy on her compulsions. The real Shaneesha was back!

Whenever her old obsessive thoughts popped up—and they always do—Shaneesha thanked her monkey and reminded herself not to give in to the urge to wash. She knew that this was a risk that most people take all the time.

I hope you will find the courage to stop avoiding, and to welcome your obsessive thoughts and the anxiety that comes with them. If you don't feel you can tackle your core fears or challenge ladder alone, don't be afraid to ask for help. (For more on the kinds of help you might get, see the appendix.) You already know where doing compulsions leads—to more obsessions. When you stop the avoidance cycle, you will be faced with nothing more than feelings—feelings that you *can* tolerate.

When you welcome your anxiety and allow yourself to feel it, your monkey's logic is going to change. It will sound more like *You accepted the thought and you are safe. The thought must not be so dangerous after all.* That's the chatter of a tame monkey, the kind you can live with without giving up your dreams.

Of course, there will always be that tiny sliver of a chance that a scary thought will come true. There will always be risk in life. But I know you'll find that living with a little uncertainty is better than living with OCD!

Chapter 12

Other Issues

Insomnia and Depression

Nighttime can be a challenging time for anxious teens. It's the time of day when there are no distractions. There's nothing to do, nothing to look at, nothing to listen to. It's a time for your body to relax and shut down. But there's one little part of you that is still working. This part never sleeps. It's burning the midnight oil, on the job 24/7 to keep you safe from harm. Yes, it's your monkey mind!

Historically there's a good reason for your monkey mind to be on the alert at night. From the dawn of time humans have been most vulnerable after dark. When an aborigine fell asleep, he was not prepared to fight or flee if attacked by a predator or hostile tribe. Listening for strange sounds and watching for movements in the dark was necessary for our ancestors' survival.

Here we are thousands of years later, and there are no saber-toothed tigers prowling in the dark, and we have sturdy walls and locked doors protecting us. Hypervigilance at night is no longer so important. But if you have a hyperactive monkey, who's extra sensitive to danger, it will find plenty of threatening things for you to worry about. *It's 1:00 a.m. and you're still awake. You'll never get to sleep! You are going to flunk your test tomorrow!* Sound familiar?

Monkey thoughts may sound compelling when you are alone in the dark in the middle of the night, but it is important to remember that the monkey mind part of your brain is designed only for spotting potential threats, not for evaluating them. Your monkey is correct about the time, and that you will not be getting as much sleep as you might want, but it can only guess about when or if you will fall asleep and about the results of your test tomorrow. Monkey thoughts are full of miscalculations—the most common of which is over/ underestimating.

Your monkey, in its concern about your getting enough sleep, always overestimates how much sleep you need to function and how poorly you are sleeping. It also underestimates how much sleep you are actually getting and how well you will cope with less than optimal sleep the next day.

There are other miscalculations here that give it away as a monkey thought. Predicting that you will never get to sleep is assuming the worst possible scenario, or *catastrophizing*, as is predicting you will flunk the test. Ignoring the sleep you actually will get is *discounting the positive*. You can review these and other monkey miscalculations in chapter 3.

Here's another monkey thought you're probably familiar with: *You're exhausted. You'd better sleep in this weekend and catch up*. But is that a monkey thought? If you've been struggling all week, not getting enough sleep, it sounds utterly sensible. If you follow that advice you'll get short-term relief for sure. But in the long run, "catching up" on sleep this way actually makes the problem worse.

Sleeping late on weekends upsets your body's internal clock. It is like flying from California to New York for two days every week. Getting up three hours later means it will be time to go to bed three hours sooner than you're ready. It's just like having jet lag.

After a week of nights spent tossing and turning, getting up at a set hour on Saturday morning is both counterintuitive and difficult. But you need to get up out of bed, regardless of how well you slept the night before. Your day may be a struggle but it will be worth it, because you'll be building up a sleep demand for that night, making it more likely that you'll get a good night's rest.

By urging you to roll away from the morning sun and pull the covers over your head, your monkey mind is miscalculating the threat, overestimating how exhausted you really are and underestimating your ability to get through the day without more sleep. It's so easy to go along with that miscalculation. After all, who wants the anxiety of facing another day not being at your best?

The problem is, if you give in to your monkey mind and sleep in, your monkey will take credit for your survival that week. It won't notice that, because of your Saturday and Sunday sleep-ins, you have trouble getting to sleep on Sunday night; and it won't notice how the whole sleepless-week, sleep-in-weekend cycle starts over again.

Saturday morning, or any morning you are tempted to sleep late, is where you stop the cycle. To succeed at this you will need to ignore your monkey. Besides the jet-lag phenomenon, here are some other examples of monkey thoughts, along with facts that will help you develop your own alternative thoughts.

Monkey thought: *You only slept five hours! You'll never win that cross-country race!*

Fact: You may do best when you get eight to nine hours of sleep. You feel well rested and you are able to concentrate normally. We call this *optimal sleep*. The other measure is *core sleep,* which is more like six hours. If you are able to get six hours of core sleep, you may not feel as good the next day, and you might be more moody or forgetful than usual, but you will perform as well on demanding tasks like sports, homework, and tests.

Alternative thought: *I won't feel great, but as long as I got my core sleep I will do just as well in my race as I would if I had gotten optimal sleep.*

Monkey thought: *You keep tossing and turning. You haven't slept a wink!*

Fact: You are getting more sleep than you think. Teens tend to underestimate how much sleep they are getting by 20 percent. That means if you think you slept only five hours, you probably actually slept around six and a half hours. Why?

There are actually five separate stages of sleep. Stages 1 and 2 are very light; you are still somewhat aware of what is going on around you. Test subjects will report being awake during these stages, but the machines measuring their brain waves showed them as definitely asleep. Stage 1 and stage 2 sleep are very important and make up almost 50 percent of your total time asleep.

Alternative thought: *Even though I can hear things and I keep having thoughts, I am probably in stage 1 or 2. I am getting more sleep than it feels like.*

Monkey thought: *You did not get even five hours of sleep last night. You're screwed!*

Fact: If you haven't gotten your core sleep for a couple of nights, your body will automatically spend more time than usual in stage 3 sleep, which is the sleep that helps you function the next day.

Alternative thought: *If it's true that I haven't been getting core sleep, I can trust my body to spend more time in the stage it needs most.*

Monkey thought: *You did not get enough sleep last night. You had better miss first period and sleep in!*

Fact: Getting up at the same time every day will help you sleep better in the long run. The more time you are awake and exposed to daylight, the more your demand for sleep will build, helping ensure a better night's rest the next night.

Alternative thought: *Sleeping in will only cause more problems later on. It is important to get up at the same time to break the cycle of insomnia that I am in.*

If you stick to your schedule for a week, your body will begin to fall into a healthy sleep pattern. Eventually you will gain enough confidence in your ability to sleep that you'll be able to indulge in a more flexible sleep schedule. And just as important, you'll be ruling the monkey instead of it ruling you!

Anxiety and Depression

Anxiety and depression are the most common mental health problems, and teens often experience both. This is because there is a cause-and-effect relationship between the two.

As you know from reading this book, when you're feeling anxious your monkey mind is coming up with a lot of reasons why you shouldn't do certain things. When you avoid doing lots of things that, in your heart, you really want to do, over time you lose your belief in your ability to do them. You feel helpless and hopeless. Lack of motivation is the defining feature of depression.

For example, if you avoid going to parties or other social events due to your social anxiety, you may begin to have thoughts like *I'll never make friends or have a boyfriend or girlfriend*. If you avoid going on trips or to events where there are crowds of people because of your anxiety or agoraphobia, you may think, *I'll have to live here with my parents and work a crummy job forever*.

If you feel too anxious, tired, or unmotivated, you are missing out on doing the things that would help you feel better. This makes you even more anxious, tired, and unmotivated. You can get trapped in a vicious cycle of not doing things that might make you feel better, and then getting more depressed and feeling even more unmotivated.

This book is all about facing your fears and gaining back your life. If you do the exercises in this book to cope with your anxiety, your depression may go away. In fact, one treatment for depression is to get the depressed person to do the things that used to give her enjoyment before she stopped doing them due to lack of motivation.

Everybody knows the principle that motivation leads to action. If you are depressed it works the other way around: action leads to motivation (which leads to more action). Put another way, action and motivation work together like eating and hunger. You are hungry, so you eat. Eating nourishes you so that you stay alive and eventually get hungry again. People who are sick and don't have an appetite are often encouraged to eat even if they don't feel like it, because the nourishment will help bring their strength back. If you want to feel motivated you will need to jump-start the cycle by taking action even when you don't feel like it.

The Five-Minute Action Exercise

Pick an activity that you have enjoyed in the past, or something that you would like to get done—something you don't feel motivated to do. It could be a physical activity like running, riding your bike, dancing, or drawing. It could also be a task like doing homework or cleaning your room. Whatever it is, take action and do it for just five minutes, no matter how tired or unmotivated you feel. If after five minutes you want to stop, then stop. But you may find that once you commit to doing something for just five minutes you feel just a tiny bit more motivated to continue. Activity is an antidepressant.

In extreme cases of depression, some teens have thoughts about killing themselves, or even make plans to do so. If you are suicidal you need to get help. Suicide is a permanent solution to a temporary problem. No matter how miserable you feel now, things *will* get better. Don't keep these thoughts and feelings to yourself! Tell a parent or friend, see your school counselor, or call a crisis line.

This goes for all teens suffering from depression. It's always a good idea to get help. Counseling and medication are effective in treating depression. See the appendix for more on how to get help.

Most adults recall their teen years as a tough time, with bodily changes, peer and school pressure, and the expectations of adulthood approaching. As an anxious teen you may be having an especially difficult time. Remember that you are not alone, and that your life is important and worth fighting for. Like anxiety, depression can be overcome.

Believe it or not, there is a bonus prize when you learn how to overcome anxiety and depression. Knowing how to jump-start your motivation by taking action will be very useful throughout your life, because no life is without setbacks and disappointments. All the tools you learn in this book are tools that you can use your whole life to get what you want and go where you want to go.

So what are you waiting for? It's time to take action!

Appendix

Getting Extra Help

Therapy and Medication

This book is a self-help book. It explains what anxiety is and how to master it so that it doesn't get in the way of doing what you want in life. But sometimes self-help is not enough. If you are having trouble following through with the exercises and challenges in this book, or if you are doing the exercises but don't seem to be moving ahead, finding a therapist to work with may be what you need.

Mastering anxiety is like learning a sport. You might read about how the game is played and what you need to practice to get good at it, and yet still need a coach. Therapists are like coaches. They work with you to develop the skills you need and give you encouragement to practice and follow through with challenges that are especially difficult.

This book is based on cognitive behavioral therapy (CBT), acceptance and commitment therapy (ACT), and mindfulness. CBT focuses on the relationship between thoughts, feelings, and actions. A CBT therapist will help you identify and challenge the monkey thoughts that are making you more anxious and change the behaviors that are making the problem worse. ACT is a type of CBT that focuses more on changing behavior and less on changing thoughts. The objective in ACT is to identify your values and goals and commit to actions that will lead you to a more rich and meaningful life. "Mindfulness" is a broad term for ancient tools for self-discovery and well-being that are becoming increasingly relevant today.

CBT and ACT are very effective for all anxiety problems. If you decide to see a therapist, look for one who is trained in CBT or ACT, so that she or he can coach you to use the skills you have learned in this book.

What to Ask a Therapist

You will want to feel comfortable with the therapist you see. You have every right to ask questions to make sure that the therapist you choose will be a good fit with you and has experience in treating the issues you want to work on.

Here is a list of questions that are good to ask in order to find a therapist who can help you:

- What is your training in cognitive behavioral therapy? (Therapists will ideally be able to talk about workshops they have taken, experienced clinicians they have trained with, organizations they belong to, and certificates they hold in CBT.)

- What is your training and background in treating anxiety? (Make sure to ask about the specific type of anxiety you have. Sometimes therapists have more experience with one kind of anxiety, such as OCD, but not as much with another, like panic.)

- How much of your current practice involves treating anxiety? (Once again, ask about your specific type.)

- Do you feel you have been effective in treating anxiety?

- What techniques do you use to treat anxiety? (Do these techniques help you identify unhelpful thoughts and steps to take to help you face your fears?)

231

- If necessary, are you willing to leave your office to help me face my fears? (Some of your challenges may require you and your therapist to enter into specific, anxiety-provoking situations.)

About Medication

If you are experiencing extreme anxiety that is getting in the way of your functioning—such as getting out of the house and going to school—or doing the exercises in this book, you may want to talk to your doctor about medications. Those who prescribe medication for anxiety are usually family doctors, general practitioners, or psychiatrists (medical doctors who specialize in mental health).

Of those who try medication, people who combine medication with CBT obtain the best results. This makes sense. The medication can help lower your overall anxiety, while the therapy teaches you skills to master the anxiety now and in the long run. That way, when you stop taking medication, you will be much less likely to experience a return of your anxiety. If you rely just on medication, when you stop taking it it's very likely your anxiety will come back.

There are basically two types of medication for treating anxiety: antidepressants and benzodiazepines.

Antidepressants

You may be wondering why antidepressants are prescribed for anxiety. The reason is that the way the drug works in your brain to decrease depression works to decrease anxiety as well. Also, as I mentioned before, it is not uncommon for people who have anxiety to have depression too. These medications can help with both problems.

The most common type of antidepressants is called selective serotonin reuptake inhibitors, or SSRIs. Serotonin is a brain chemical that influences mood, and these drugs work by increasing serotonin levels. They also work on other chemicals in the brain that affect mood. Common SSRIs include Prozac, Paxil, Celexa, Zoloft, Lexapro, and Luvox. Other antidepressants that are sometimes used are Effexor, Cymbalta, Serzone, and Remeron.

SSRIs have pros and cons.

Pros:

- Most people find it easy to take pills.

- These medications are not addictive.

- Because you take these medications every day, as opposed to just when you feel anxious, they are less likely to be used as a way to avoid anxiety.

Cons:

- There can be side effects. The most common are nausea, diarrhea, constipation, drowsiness, jitteriness, dry mouth, headaches, shakiness, and sexual effects such as decreased sex drive or difficulty having an orgasm. Many of these side effects decrease over time.

- These medications can take from four to eight weeks to have a noticeable effect.

- Going off the medication can cause uncomfortable symptoms, such as dizziness, nausea, difficulty sleeping, or flu-like symptoms. If you decrease the dose slowly under a doctor's direction when going off these medications, these effects will be less intense.

- When you stop taking these medications, anxiety symptoms usually come back.

Benzodiazepines

Benzodiazepines are relaxants that work very quickly in the body and brain. People usually take them when they become anxious or panicky, or when they are going into situations that make them anxious.

Common benzodiazepines include Xanax, Valium, Ativan, and Klonopin.

There are pros and cons to taking benzodiazepines.

Pros:

- They are quick-acting.

- They can be taken as needed.

- They are not very expensive.

- Most people find it easy to take a pill.

Cons:

- There can be side effects, such as drowsiness, light-headedness, confusion, and depression.

- They can be deadly if you mix them with alcohol.

- They can be physically addicting.

- You can become dependent on them and use them as a way to avoid your anxiety. They can get in the way of facing your fears and gaining confidence in yourself.

Jennifer Shannon, LMFT, is author of *The Shyness and Social Anxiety Workbook for Teens* and cofounder of the Santa Rosa Center for Cognitive-Behavioral Therapy in Santa Rosa, CA. She is a diplomate of the Academy of Cognitive Therapy.

Illustrator **Doug Shannon** is a freelance cartoonist.

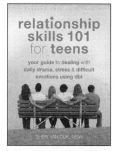

Register your **new harbinger** titles for additional benefits!

When you register your **new harbinger** title—purchased in any format, from any source—you get access to benefits like the following:

- Downloadable accessories like printable worksheets and extra content

- Instructional videos and audio files

- Information about updates, corrections, and new editions

Not every title has accessories, but we're adding new material all the time.

Access free accessories in 3 easy steps:

1. Sign in at NewHarbinger.com (or **register** to create an account).

2. Click on **register a book**. Search for your title and click the **register** button when it appears.

3. Click on the **book cover or title** to go to its details page. Click on **accessories** to view and access files.

That's all there is to it!

If you need help, visit:

NewHarbinger.com/accessories

new harbinger
CELEBRATING
40 YEARS